Presented to:

_____

By:

_____

Date:

_____

Life Lessons from Baseball

HONOR **HB** BOOKS

Inspiration and Motivation for the Seasons of Life

COOK COMMUNICATIONS MINISTRIES
Colorado Springs, Colorado • Paris, Ontario
KINGSWAY COMMUNICATIONS, LTD.
Eastbourne, England

Honor Books is an imprint of
Cook Communications Ministries, Colorado Springs, CO 80918
Cook Communications, Paris, Ontario
Kingsway Communications, Eastbourne, England

Life Lessons from Baseball
© 2004 by VisionQuest Communications Group, Inc.

Printed in the United States of America

2 3 4 5 6 7 8 9 Printing/Year 09 08 07 06

Developed by Bordon Books

Manuscript written by Steve Riach, Dallas, Texas

ISBN 1-56292-994-1

Contents

Foreword:

Baseball is a game that captures us all. While championships are played out in modern stadiums with millions of dollars on the line, the essence of the game comes down to a simple passion. The same passion that grips a boy with a ball and a bat on a sandlot, today grips every man wearing a big league uniform. It is the game itself and what that game builds into you which makes baseball so captivating.

Throughout the history of this great game, players have learned some of their most valuable life lessons in the midst of that very atmosphere. Each day they faced the prospect of success, failure, the unexpected, the undesired, and the overexposed. With all of that constantly coming at you, let me tell you, players do learn to deal with a wide variety of experiences.

For pitchers, so many of those experiences relate to life. There are times when they make their very best pitch, and it is hit out of the ballpark. Other times a favorite pitch may not bring about the same response from an umpire. On other occasions their best effort still results in a loss, or a performance in which the pitcher is not at their best is still good enough for a win. I have experienced all of these.

The amazing contradictions in the game of baseball can be summed up in a feeling with which all players are familiar–Even while standing on the mound with the ball in your hand and a lead on the scoreboard, you are struck by the stark realization that so much of the game is out of your control. Really, all you can control are your preparation, your effort, and your mental approach. So I gave my full attention to those areas, and remembered that I could not control the rest.

Isn't that how life is? We can't control anything beyond our preparation, effort, and outlook. The rest, including our destiny and how that destiny plays out, is in much bigger hands.

I feel blessed to have worn a major league uniform for twenty-seven years and honored to have records attached to my name. Yet the one thing I am most proud of about my career is that most people remember me as much for my character as they do for anything I accomplished on the field. I can't think of a better way to be remembered.

It was my mission to give the very best possible effort every time I stepped across those white lines. It was also my conviction that I was there to help make those around me better if I could, and to live a life before teammates and fans that gave them a reason to cheer even when I may not have pitched so well. I'm thankful I had that opportunity. All of the records in the game can't measure up to knowing I had a positive influence on others.

Baseball tests and reveals a man's character. In some instances, it also helps to shape that character. There is growth in failure, and responsibility in success. Teamwork is critical; communication and sacrifice are necessities. Responsibility is demanded, leadership recognized, and self-control vital. No matter how awful one game goes, redemption can always be found the very next day. Through it all, one can realize a new perspective, an understanding of priorities, and a true sense of purpose.

The moments that occur in baseball are more than just experiences. They are the basis for life lessons; just like those you will read about in this book. On these pages, Steve Riach has compiled compelling stories from the great game of baseball that will serve as an inspiration to you. Whether you are an avid fan or casual observer, through the real life experiences of the people you will read about here you will find a way in which you can view your own life experiences. *Life Lessons from Baseball* is not just a collection of stories about America's pastime. Rather, it is a kind of handbook for life. This book presents models of faith and character along with time-tested truths and practical applications to help you succeed at life's most important game so that you can become a true champion.

NOLAN RYAN
1999 Baseball Hall of Fame Inductee
Holder of 53 Major League Records
Eight time All-Star
324 victories
5,714 strikeouts
7 no-hitters

Profile of FELIPE ALOU

*"The bottom line of why
we believe we have
been successful with
the development
of players—
and of men—
is because
of love."*

LEADERSHIP:

A champion mentors from experience.

The year was 1956, nine years after Jackie Robinson broke in with the Brooklyn Dodgers and integrated baseball, a year that would forever shape Felipe Alou's approach to people. Alou found himself on a bus one night, heading through the Louisiana night. He sat in the bus's backseat, at that time still the only seat for a black man traveling in a public vehicle from a place like Lake Charles, Louisiana, to a destination like Cocoa Beach, Florida.

Alou, almost twenty-one, had only recently discovered he was black. His father, Don Abundio was black. His mother, Doña Virginia, whose father had emigrated from Spain, was white. Felipe had never thought much about skin color until he came to the United States from Santo Domingo in the Dominican Republic. Now he was forced to confront it.

In his first professional baseball season in the States, he had had just nine at-bats in five games before officials of his Lake Charles team realized that discrimination laws in area cities prohibited Alou from playing there. That was why Alou was packed into the rear of a bus on the way to the Florida State League. Thus, the legacy of the Alous began.

Felipe was the first of three brothers brought to the U.S. He arrived a year before middle brother Mateo and three years before the youngest sibling, Jesus. They would become the first set of three brothers in major league history ever to play in the same outfield together, when they did so for the San Francisco Giants in 1963. Many other Alous followed. Felipe's four sons all played the game, including Moises, who has been in the majors since 1992, when his father managed him with the Montreal Expos. There are countless nephews and cousins who have had a taste of pro ball as well. Sooner or later, it seems, Alous will play baseball.

Felipe made the Giants team during the 1958 season, the second Dominican-born player in the major leagues (The Giants had called up Ozzie Virgil two years earlier, but Virgil had grown up in New York). He hit .275 in his second full year, but when a sportswriter praised him, he said, "Wait till you see my brother." Matty arrived in the majors in 1960, Jesus in 1963.

On September 10, 1963, San Francisco was playing the New York Mets at the Polo Grounds. Felipe was the Giants' starting right fielder. Matty and Jesus entered the game as pinch hitters and stayed in to play center field and left field, respectively. For the only time in the history of baseball, three brothers were playing on the same team in the same major league game.

When they played in the U.S. as part of the first contingent of Dominican players, they not only opened the door for many great stars to follow, but they also became stars in their own right.

Together the brothers finished with 5,094 hits among them— second most in history among brothers, about 500 fewer than the Waner brothers, and 241 more than the DiMaggios.

Felipe, however, has always been the leader, a natural role for him. Today he has solidified his reputation as one of the top managers in baseball. Since 1992 he has consistently taken young, inexperienced teams and turned them into competitive groups while also developing them as solid individuals. In Montreal, Detroit, and San Francisco, it has been paramount for Felipe to treat every player as if he were his own son.

"The bottom line of why we believe we have been successful with the development of players—and of men—is because of love," says Alou. "Trying to follow the words of the Lord about loving your neighbor. And we have shown people love and respect. We care about their baseball career; we care about their personal life, about their domestic life, about their spiritual life. When you come into an atmosphere like that, I believe chances are that you are going to believe what they teach you. We've always had that vision of teaching, not only baseball, but teaching men, so that when they leave here they can be an example for young people."

The Heart of a Champion calls on personal experience in relating to others:

Felipe Alou lived through enough racial strife to make any man cold and bitter. But Alou turned the personal pain into benchmarks for his future. Alou is a beloved manager to those who play for him because they know he genuinely cares. Not only a respected strategist, he is also a man of compassion, a combination that makes him a great leader. Alou's early experiences helped establish how he would treat his players—the way he wished he had been treated.

All truly great leaders, whether on the playing field, on the battlefield, or in the boardroom, have one common trait: they care about people. Strategies, theories, principles, and slogans have never truly won the hearts of people. But when a man or woman demonstrates how much they care, they lay the groundwork for success. Leaders cannot intimidate or legislate people into action without an eventual organizational collapse. But when leadership arises out of love, truth, compassion, integrity, respect, and excellence—following the leadership example of Jesus Christ—the groups they lead will withstand any adversity.

"My command is this: Love each other as I have loved. . . .
I no longer call you servants, because a servant does
not know his master's business. Instead, I have
called you friends, for everything that I learned
from my Father I have made known to you."

—John 15:12,15

"I think the best things in life are to live simply and to give from your heart."

GENEROSITY:

A champion gives unselfishly.

hird baseman Tony Batista is known in baseball circles for his unorthodox batting stance. One day in February 1998, while playing winter ball in Venezuela, Batista wanted to try something new to give his hitting a boost. He came up with a new stance that basically opened up his legs completely, with his chest facing the pitcher. This right-handed batter spreads out his legs on nearly an even plane, with his left leg almost facing the third base dugout. It looks nearly impossible for him to be ready for the pitch in such an open stance. But it has worked for Batista. From 1999 through 2002, he has hit at least 25 home runs each year. In 2002 he was the Baltimore Orioles' lone representative on the American League All-Star Team.

"I tried to do something different," he says of the new stance, "and right away I got a hit with that kind of stance. It's been working for me since that day."

Batista became interested in baseball as a child growing up in Puerta Plata, Dominican Republic, watching his two older brothers, Ramirez and Vicente, play the game. "I saw them going to the stadium to play, so I decided to go with them and try to learn. And they taught me. My first manager was [the youngest of my two older brothers], when I was nine years old. He had a team, and he put me into the games. And I learned from them. They both were professional players in the states, but they got only to Double-A."

Batista signed with the Oakland A's as a non-drafted free agent in 1991 at the age of seventeen. Although his brothers and one sister had left home before him, Batista says the departure was very difficult for his parents. His family is still in the Dominican Republic, so Batista keeps up regular communication through e-mail and telephone.

Baseball was not all that Batista learned from his brothers. He also was taught about faith. His relationship with Jesus Christ, Batista says, means much more to him than his baseball career.

To reinforce this relationship, he has committed himself to an action that his brothers also taught him: making donations to the church. Since 1998, when he was playing for the Arizona Diamondbacks, Batista has been making unannounced visits to churches in cities across the United States and giving them financial donations from his earnings as a big leaguer.

Batista regularly spreads 10 percent of his $4 million salary to various needy churches, both in the Dominican Republic, his homeland, and in poor sections of the town where the team is playing on the road.

He has been known to take a taxi to a Christian church in an impoverished area so that he can make a sizeable donation. During the 2002 season, he took a taxi to a downtown church in Kansas City to present them with a check for $16,000. He does all this without a media following or publicity. It is not a staged show of goodwill, but rather an outflow of his heart.

"I go to different churches in different cities," he explains. "God is the one who tells me which churches to visit for making donations. The one who blesses me is Jesus Christ.

"I think it's more important than throwing a no-hitter. I think it's more important than hitting seven home runs in one game. I think it's more important than that. It's more important to me.

"The best thing I feel happy about is my life with Jesus Christ. He continues to bless me, and I continue to live as a simple guy. Sometimes when you get blessings, you become rich and famous. And sometimes you forget about where the blessing comes from.

But that's the best thing I carry in my mind. I don't forget where the blessing comes from and where I come from. I think the best things in life are to live simply and to give from your heart."

The Heart of a Champion gives out of a cheerful heart to bless others:

Tony Batista may not be considered a "superstar" in baseball, but to those he has helped, he is the embodiment of unselfish compassion. The most remarkable aspect of Batista's story is that he attempts to keep his actions completely discreet and gives because he is thankful for what he has been given.

Why do you give? Is it for tax purposes? Out of a sense of guilt? To gain attention? Is it out of a desire to receive? Or is it merely to express your gratitude to God? Many tell us that the formula for getting is giving. It is true that God blesses those who give, but will He bless those who are motivated to give only because they want to get something back? Is the kingdom of God some sort of spiritual investment portfolio? Well, yes and no. If you give from a heart that seeks only to get back material wealth, at some point it will all cave in on you. Perhaps you will be blessed materially, but there will still be an unfulfilled hole in your soul. But if you give because you want to bless God and others, what you receive in return will be far greater than the monetary value and will bring the greatest return.

Each man should give what he has decided in his heart to give, not reluctantly or under compulsion, for God loves a cheerful giver. And God is able to make all grace abound to you, so that in all things at all times, having all that you need, you will abound in every good work.

—2 Corinthians 9:7-8

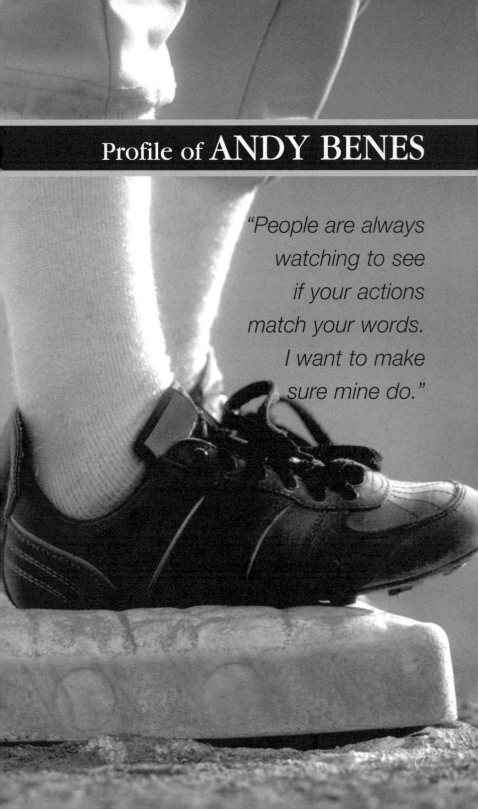

"People are always watching to see if your actions match your words. I want to make sure mine do."

INTEGRITY:

Champions keep their word.

T rades are a regular part of professional sports. A player and his family are secure one minute; the next they are facing an upheaval of major proportions. Emotions rise to the top, both good and bad.

With the July 31, 1995, major league baseball trade deadline just hours away, the Seattle Mariners and San Diego Padres consummated a late trade. The Padres sent veteran ace pitcher Andy Benes and a player to be named later to Seattle in exchange for young pitcher Ron Villone and outfield prospect Marc Newfield.

Amid the emotional chaos of knowing he would soon be trying to get to know new teammates in the midst of a pressure-packed pennant race, Benes still had some unfinished items to resolve.

On August 1, the day after he was traded, Benes walked into the Padres corporate offices and delivered a check for $10,000 (dated August 1) for the Padres Scholars Program.

The Padres' vice president of public affairs, Dr. Charles Steinberg, was shocked, not by the amount but by the man fulfilling his commitment.

"He gave money that was matched by the owners, money that four kids would benefit from," explains Dr. Steinberg.

"It was a gesture he didn't have to make because he had been traded. Nobody would have held it against him if he had said, 'Look, I've been traded now, and I'm not part of this.' Instead, he said, 'I like the program, I like what we've started here, and this is still my community.'"

Benes' contribution meant that four middle-school-age kids would each receive a $5,000 scholarship. The impact that Benes' generosity has made on the lives of those four young people is only now being realized, but his integrity impacted Steinberg in a great way.

"The impressions that players make on you are the impressions they make on you as people," says Steinberg. "We watch them, and we love their athletic performance; but your memories of them wind up being gestures like this, rather than the shutout or the strikeout. These are the things that judge a guy's character far more than anything that goes on out on the baseball field. . . . It was one of the greatest things I've seen in my years in baseball."

Benes was baseball's number-one draft pick by the Padres in 1988 and has had a solid career despite battling nagging injuries. He has pitched on contenders in San Diego, Seattle, and St. Louis. Still, his greatest contribution has been his commitment to using his platform to help others, the way he did following his 1995 trade. His peers know him as a man of his word.

Benes' friend, former major league pitcher Don Gordon, says Andy's desire to reach out is pure. "He's off the charts as far as community involvement. He's community-minded, but not for personal gain. Andy does it out of the goodness of his heart."

"I want people to see something different in me through my example," said Benes. "People are always watching to see if your actions match your words. I want to make sure mine do."

The Heart of a Champion keeps its word in all circumstances:

Andy Benes' example of integrity is unique in today's world. He made a commitment, while a member of the Padres, to help the team's surrounding community. Once he was traded, most assumed he was released from the obligation. Not Benes. The pitcher was determined to fulfill the promise he had made, simply because he had made the promise. Benes has been a solid pitcher for a number of teams during his career. More importantly, he has been a true example of character. His commitment to his word in 1995 helped four needy students receive an education and gave a generation of baseball players an example of integrity.

What is it about keeping our word that is so difficult for people today? So many people are challenged to be where they say they will be and do what they say they will do. Most look for loopholes when fulfilling their word means having to give of their time, energy, or resources. At times our attitude is that if we can possibly get out of it, we'll look for a way to do so. What if God took the same approach to His relationship with us? What if His promises were conditional, and He fulfilled His Word only when He felt like it? Rather, God is the same yesterday, today, and forever, and His promises are the same for everyone who chooses to believe on Him. What do you do when you give your word? Do you go out of your way to make sure you fulfill your promises? Or do you look for a way out? Integrity means keeping your word—no matter what.

"When a man makes a vow to the LORD or takes an oath to obligate himself by a pledge, he must not break his word but must do everything he said."

—Numbers 30:2

"I wasn't really afraid because God allowed me to be at peace. . . . "

SACRIFICE:

A champion is willing to love sacrificially.

When Terry Blocker was asked to become a replacement player for the Atlanta Braves during the baseball strike of 1995, the onetime big league outfielder was not thinking it would be his ticket back to the majors. Rather, he had another agenda.

Blocker, who has spent the better part of nine years in baseball as a minor league player and portions of three years in the big leagues with the Braves, had been retired since 1993. Money and a last chance at fame were never his objectives. Blocker went into spring training with a sense of duty. He had one final opportunity to share what he felt was a vital message with the other players. He wanted to tell them about faith in Christ.

After one spring training practice at the Braves complex in West Palm Beach, Florida, Blocker approached a teammate, thirty-year-old pitcher Dave Shotkoski. Blocker asked Shotkoski if he had time to talk with him about his faith. Shotkoski, a husband and the father of an eight-month-old daughter, said he was interested in talking, but he had to take care of some family financial obligations. He told Blocker he would be happy to talk with him the following day.

For Dave Shotkoski, the next day never came.

Just hours after speaking with Blocker, Shotkoski was murdered in a robbery attempt in West Palm Beach. News of the murder floored Blocker. He knew he had to do something.

"When I was told about the death by some other teammates, I cried," recalls Blocker, who is also a husband and father. "I was just witnessing to him, and I don't even know whether or not he had accepted Jesus. I prayed to see if there was anything I could do."

Blocker discovered there was something that he could do, and he was determined to try. He decided to help find the killer.

Although he knew how dangerous it could be, Blocker proceeded, against the counsel of friends, disregarding the danger to his own well-being.

The search took Blocker to some of the meanest streets in West Palm Beach, where he eventually approached a young drug dealer, seeking information. The drug dealer was not in a mood to comply. He threatened Blocker's life, but Blocker remained undeterred.

"Once I started talking to this guy, and he saw that I was a Christian, I gained his respect," says Blocker. "I even talked to him about Jesus, and he told me he'd have to think about what I said. He did tell me that if he found out anything he'd let me know. I wasn't really afraid because God allowed me to be at peace during the confrontation. That's how I knew I could do something about this terrible tragedy to a teammate."

The next day the murderer was overheard bragging about the killing to several people—one of them the man Blocker had spoken with. He promptly called Blocker, who informed the Braves. Eventually an arrest was made, and Dave Shotkoski's killer was apprehended.

The Heart of a Champion willfully sacrifices to help the cause of others:

Terry Blocker had an undistinguished major league career. Few outside of Atlanta have ever heard of him. Yet what he did for the family of Dave Shotkoski will not be forgotten. Only God knows the outcome of Dave Shotkoski's eternal standing and the impact Blocker's words had on him. But Blocker's impact in the Shotkoski family is clear. By risking his own life, he was the key to a murderer being taken off the streets, an act that helped the Shotkoski family bring closure to their tragic situation.

Blocker's example of courage and sacrifice are startling in a "me first" age. Yet his actions demonstrate the character of a true hero. What would you do if you were in Terry Blocker's situation? How important to you is the life of another? God wants us to feel His heart for the preciousness of human life. Every moment we have in relationship with another should be used to demonstrate the love of God to that one, in word and deed. Blocker did this, even to the point of risking his life. Will you love others in the same way?

"My command is this:
Love each other as I have loved you."

—John 15:12

"I've been spit on, had beer thrown on me and been sworn at, and was hit eleven times out of eleven at-bats while in college. But the memories I have are the ovations when I would run in from the bull pen."

PERSEVERANCE:

A champion is undeterred by others.

All her life, Ila Borders was told that she would never be able to do it. She was told that her dream was ridiculous. That she should give up this wild idea and go back to doing things girls are supposed to do. She endured verbal abuse from fans, snickers from teammates, catcalls from opponents, and mockery from the media. Yet Ila never lost sight of her dream. And in the realization of that dream, she never lost her self-respect.

In 1997 Borders became the first female to play men's professional baseball when she pitched for the St. Paul Saints of the Northern League. Borders' historic moment came on May 31, 1997, when, as a relief pitcher, she entered a game against Sioux Falls. She recorded her first pro victory later that year and helped the Duluth-Superior Dukes to the league championship with a 1.97 earned run average.

Borders continued to play professionally through the 2000 season, when she announced her retirement. A media circus marked her professional career at times, surrounding her and running rampant with tabloid-type stories about ulterior motives behind Borders' effort to crack the pro ranks. Nonplussed, Borders steadfastly told reporters she played the game for one reason only.

"I'll look back and say I did something nobody ever did," said Borders. "I'm proud of that. I wasn't out to prove women's rights or anything. I love baseball. Ask a guy if he's doing it to prove men's rights. He'll say he's doing because he loves the game."

A high school baseball star in Southern California, Borders was Whittier Christian High School's Most Valuable Player (MVP). She became the first woman ever to earn a scholarship to play men's collegiate baseball when she was signed to a letter of intent by Vanguard University (formerly Southern California College).

While her physical attributes did not equal those of her peers in the Northern League, Borders succeeded through intelligence, composure, and strength of will.

"She threw a fastball probably 72 to 73 mph, and her curveball maybe 58 mph. Most everybody has to throw an 87- to 88-mph fastball and a curveball at least 77 to 78 mph," said Borders' manager, Mike Littlewood of the Zion (Utah) Pioneerzz (*sic*), during her final pro season. "She knew how to pitch."

Because of that and what she had to endure, Littlewood says Borders should be judged by different standards than other baseball players. "Ila was one of the most courageous people I've ever met or seen play the game," said Littlewood.

In her three years in the game, Borders dealt with prurient inquiries from the press—no, she did not shower with the guys—and outright harassment from fans.

"I've been spit on, had beer thrown on me and been sworn at, and was hit eleven times out of eleven at bats while in college," Borders said upon her retirement. "But the memories I have are the ovations when I would run in from the bull pen."

Through it all, Borders never lost perspective on what she had accomplished, nor her sense of identity: "I happen to think it's pretty fantastic that I'm the only female to ever play baseball with the guys."

The Heart of a Champion is not discouraged by the opinions of others:

Ila Borders faced a difficult road to walk in pursuing her dream. As the only female attempting to play professional baseball, not only were the odds against her but also most of the media and baseball-following public. The treatment she endured was similar to that of Jackie Robinson fifty years earlier. She faced derision for no reason other than her gender. Yet Borders stood firm in the midst of overwhelming opposition and pursued the dream God had placed in her heart. She did not let the opinions or derogatory remarks of others stop her. Because she pressed on in the face of opposition, Borders made history and became a trailblazer for others.

The old saying "Sticks and stones may break my bones, but words will never hurt me" is one of the most profoundly untrue statements ever uttered. While physical harm is painful, no one thing has caused more widespread damage to more individuals than words. Plain and simple, words or the lack of words have inflicted many emotional wounds that are slow to heal. Many of us have heard constantly what we will never become. Anyone can tell you what you are not, but Jesus came to tell you who you are. Do you know who you are? Are you shaped by the words spoken over you by humans or by the Word of God? God's Word explicitly proclaims that you are His beloved, and that He shouts with great joy about you, sings over you, and dances with great rejoicing as He thinks of you. While this is hard for us to imagine, it is true. God loves you just as you are. He wants you to know how He feels about you and see yourself in that light, rather than in light of what others say about you. Which will you receive?

"The LORD your God is with you, he is mighty to save.
He will take great delight in you, he will quiet you
with his love, he will rejoice over you with singing."

—Zephaniah 3:17

Profile of TIM BURKE

"Baseball will do just fine without me. It's not going to miss a beat. But I'm the only father my children have. I'm the only husband my wife has. And they need me a lot worse than baseball does."

SACRIFICE:

A champion sacrifices for others.

B aseball was the center of Tim Burke's universe from the time he first played Little League ball in Omaha, Nebraska, at age seven, and throughout his eight years in the major leagues. But in 1993 things suddenly changed.

Tim was at spring training with his new team, the Cincinnati Reds, ready to begin his ninth big league season. But just a few days after reporting to camp, he had a change of heart. On February 27 Tim walked into the office of Reds Manager Tony Perez and General Manager Jim Bowden and told them he was retiring.

At age 34 he walked away from a six-figure contract and the game he loved for something he loved even more—his family. Tim's decision had nothing to do with performance, injuries, or contract disputes. Rather, Tim Burke walked away from the game of baseball to spend more time with his wife, Christine, and their four adopted special-needs children. As Tim saw it, the kids didn't need a baseball star. They needed a full-time daddy.

That Tim walked away from the game was amazing. That he quit when he did was altogether stunning. Tim was at the height of his career. He had become one of the game's premier relief pitchers in his eight years with the Expos, Mets, and Yankees, collecting 49 wins and 102 saves, and 2 shutout innings pitched in the 1989 all-star game.

Profile of Tim Burke

Walking away meant leaving behind a $650,000-a-year salary and likely additional millions in the years to follow. But money didn't matter; neither did fame. Tim's heart wasn't at the ballpark anymore. It was at home. "Baseball will do just fine without me," Burke told reporters as he left the Reds camp. "It's not going to miss a beat. But I'm the only father my children have. I'm the only husband my wife has. And they need me a lot worse than baseball does."

The choice to give up the game was made easy when Tim looked at what he was going home to. The Burke's first child, Stephanie, was a premature infant they had adopted from South Korea. Next came Ryan from Guatemala—he suffered from a thyroid disorder. Then Nicole, also from Korea, arrived with a serious heart defect and a missing right hand. Finally came Wayne, a Vietnamese orphan born with a clubfoot and hepatitis B. Tim had a home team to which he was eager to give his love in the same way he had given himself to the game—with his whole heart. "Christine and I both have a lot of love to give away and feel that children are the ideal ones to receive it," Tim said.

In 1989 the Burkes had planned to pick up Ryan from Guatemala during the all-star break. Four days before the trip, Tim learned he had been named to his first all-star team. Christine insisted that he play. So, after pitching two shutout innings, Tim caught a midnight flight from Los Angeles to Guatemala City, arriving at 6:00 A.M. to join his wife and new son. But it was Nicole's serious health problems that first opened the door to Tim's departure from baseball. Just one day prior to Nicole's (then ten months old) open-heart surgery, Tim was traded from Montreal to the Mets. He had to leave for New York while Nicole was in serious condition, leaving Christine to handle the situation alone. Nicole subsequently suffered brain damage from the operation. "It's easy to be irresponsible. I was not responsible," says Tim. "Christine was the leader. She took care of the kids; she was their teacher and leader. She had to take care of the finances, and she had to move us—thirty-eight times in ten years."

Tim wanted that to change, but he would have to pay a price to see it happen, a price that to Tim seems insignificant the longer he is away from baseball. Since his retirement, he has had no regrets, for the reward has come in fours, emphasized every time Stephanie and Ryan tell people, "My daddy retired from baseball because he loves us so much."

The Heart of a Champion gives up what is important for who is more important:

Tim Burke made sport's ultimate sacrifice. At the height of his career, he walked away for the sake of his family. Burke was making millions and enjoying the advantages that come with being a professional athlete; yet he missed out on what happened at home with his growing family. He missed seeing his adopted children change every day. He missed experiencing family life together with his wife. So he gave up what was good for something better. Burke decided not to let his career get in the way of his family. For him, choosing family was clearly choosing the "best" thing. Could he have taken the same type of action without giving up baseball? Most likely not, but Burke was not willing to risk losing one more day with his family to find out.

Good is the enemy of best. We realize how true this statement is as we consider how often our preoccupation with things that are good keeps us from the best things God has for us. Indeed, when we settle for things that are good, we always miss out on the best. Are you satisfied with having a "good" marriage? "Good" relationships? A "good" walk with God? Or do you seek the best? For Tim Burke, the best wasn't earning big contracts and making all-star teams; rather, it was raising his children and loving his wife in the way each needed him. Don't settle for the good. God wants you to have the best that He has for you. Go for God's best—the reward will be much greater than the cost.

Husbands, love your wives, just as Christ loved the church and gave himself up for her.

—Ephesians 5:25

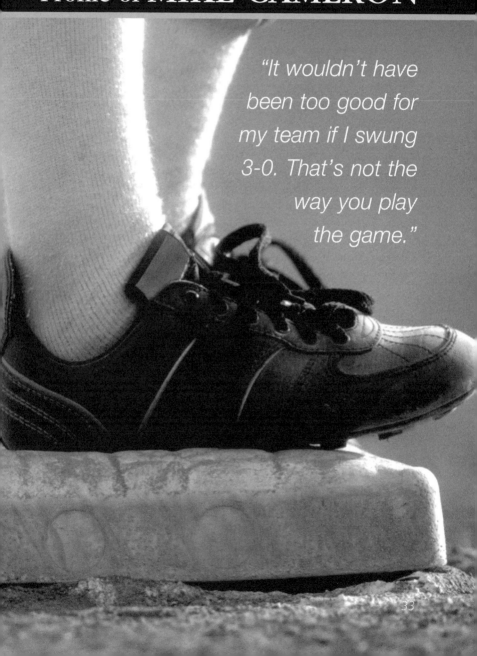

"It wouldn't have been too good for my team if I swung 3-0. That's not the way you play the game."

HONOR:

A champion never humiliates others.

During the 2002 season, Mike Cameron did something that only twelve other major league players had done before him. And then he did something even rarer.

On May 2, 2002, in a game against the Chicago White Sox in Chicago, Cameron hit four home runs in a single game. He came within a few feet of hitting a fifth.

A Gold Glove Award-winning center fielder, Cameron had made a name for himself with his sparkling defense throughout his career, along with being known as the man to take the place of Ken Griffey Jr. as the center fielder in Seattle. He has been known to make highlight reels most often for taking away home runs with outstanding catches, often reaching over the center field wall. But on this night it was Cameron's bat that made others take notice . . . and his character.

He hit his four homers in his first four at-bats and had two chances to hit a fifth. He was hit by a pitch in the seventh inning, and he flied out to deep right field in the ninth, coming within a few feet of becoming the first player ever to hit five home runs in a single nine-inning game. He was looking for history, but not at the expense of sportsmanship.

In his final at bat in the ninth, Cameron's character was on display. He had the opportunity to swing at a 3-balls-0-strikes pitch from Sox reliever Mike Porzio, which he knew would be a fastball right over the plate and in the hitting zone. But, with his team up by 11 runs, he took the pitch for a strike.

"I really wanted to make it happen, but I didn't want to swing at that 3-0 pitch, because I didn't want to make my team look bad," Cameron said, although he felt it was the pitch that could have been home run number five.

Instead of going for the record, Cameron chose decorum and the epitome of sportsmanship. The unwritten edict agreed upon among major league players is not swinging at a 3-0 pitch when your team is blowing out the opponent. After watching the 3-0 pitch, Cameron fouled off a 3-1 pitch, and then hit a liner to the warning track in right field. He was nonplussed about the opportunity missed. "It wouldn't have been too good for my team if I swung on a 3-0. That's not the way you play the game."

Following the Mariners 15-4 victory over the White Sox, Cameron had a difficult time getting back to the clubhouse. Teammates made him wear a makeshift cape and crown that read "King Cam 5-2-02." As he walked in he went through a human tunnel of cheering teammates.

"The guys made me feel like the king of the hill," Cameron said of his monumental night.

The display of character and humility in the midst of his career night was emblematic of what has made Cameron an extremely popular player among teammates and opponents. White Sox Manager Jerry Manuel, who managed Cameron during his days as a Sox player in 1999, said of Cameron after the game, "You have to applaud the young man. You have to be excited for Mike. He's a tremendous young man. He gave us everything he had when he was here."

Said White Sox General Manager Ken Williams after the game of Cameron's choice to not show up the opponent, "I thought it was Mike Cameron showing his class."

The Heart of a Champion refuses to benefit personally at the expense of the dignity of others:

Mike Cameron's display of sportsmanship in a "me first" society is startling. In an age when every big highlight is replayed multiple times on sports news programs coast-to-coast, it is common to see athletes trying hard to become the lead story. The 3-0 pitch to Cameron undoubtedly gave him the best chance of making history. That he didn't take it shows that he is a man of honor, who was unwilling to sacrifice his teammates—the unwritten rule of conduct among players—or his own reputation for personal glory.

What does it mean to consider others above yourself? How does that concept materialize? When the personal honor or dignity of others is pitted against your own individual benefit, how do you respond? When we benefit at the expense of others, it often leaves us feeling unfulfilled. We were not created to humiliate or embarrass others. When our actions or words do hurt others, we compromise our own honor and integrity. It is one thing to have a passion to win or succeed. It is another to allow that passion to dehumanize others. Keep your passion and ambition in check, never sacrifice honor for glory, and you will truly come out a winner.

Do nothing out of selfish ambition or vain conceit,
but in humility consider others better than yourselves.
Each of you should look not only to your own
interests, but also to the interests of others. Your
attitude should be the same as that of Christ Jesus.

—Philippians 2:3-5

Profile of SEAN CASEY

"My faith in God really helped me through that [injury] because baseball really became a side note. . . . And I realized that circumstances happen in your life and sometimes you don't know why they happen, and you're patient to make it through whatever He has in store for you."

HONOR:

A champion has a good reputation.

I n nearly every city in which the Cincinnati Reds play, Sean Casey is referred to as "The Mayor." This is because the Reds first baseman is known by his peers as *the nicest man in baseball*. Go to any National League city and ask any player who in baseball is the most personable, affable, and polite, and they will nearly unanimously tell you it is Casey. It's not hard to figure out why. He is known to spend countless hours shaking hands with teammates, opponents, fans, clubhouse attendants, groundskeepers, and autograph seekers. When interrupted at dinner by adoring fans, he commonly puts his utensils down and engages in conversation. He gives his time in the community, is helpful to the media, and calls nearly everyone by their first name. Reds shortstop Barry Larkin calls him "the most sincere, honest, hardworking American I know."

Says Reds pitcher Danny Graves, "There's nobody like him. He's the nicest guy in baseball. Sean's 'the Mayor' in every city we go to. We could be in Hackensack, and he'd have people coming up to him saying hello—and he remembers everybody's name."

On the first day of spring training one year, Casey pulled up at the Reds' complex in Sarasota, Florida, and walked into the pressroom to approach the Cincinnati beat writers and welcome them to camp. In 1999 he called *Dayton Daily News* writer Hal McCoy and congratulated him on his wedding day.

Profile of Sean Casey

"He's the most polite and kindhearted player I have met in all my years of covering baseball," says McCoy. "His memory is incredible. No matter who you are, if he talks to you once, he'll remember your name every time he sees you."

"I want to make people feel welcome," says Casey. "I try not to share much anger or negative emotion. My father taught me to treat people the way I want to be treated."

Casey has been that way since he was a pudgy kid who battled migraine headaches while growing up in Upper St. Clair, Pennsylvania. He is infamous for striking up conversations with opposing runners while he is holding them on first base. He is everybody's friend. Once after Pittsburgh's Al Martin singled, Casey struck up a conversation with him, wishing him well in reference to trade rumors that had swirled around Martin. While Casey encouraged him, Martin finally interrupted, saying, "Excuse me, but I think I'll steal second base." To which Casey responded, "If anyone can do it, you can." The stunned Martin spoke with reporters about the incident after the game, saying, "I've never had anyone talk to me like that. The amazing thing about it is, he is sincere." Others like Mark McGwire and Mark Grace have told the media of similar conversations.

Such is the way of Sean Casey. He is involved in Big Brothers, has reached out to sick children and adults alike, and, according to their testimonies, has made their lives better.

Once he struck up a friendship with a Dayton pizza parlor manager named Shane Whiteman, whom he met in the players' parking lot after a game. Several weeks into their friendship, Whiteman approached Casey in the parking lot after a game. Whiteman's stepfather had died, and the family did not have the money to cover funeral costs. Casey reached for his wallet and offered to pay the expenses, but Whiteman declined. So Casey offered to sign autographs at a trading card shop to raise the money, and the bill was covered.

Says Casey's father, Jim, of the incident, which is ever indicative of his son's character, "You know, he didn't want that story to get in the press. When Sean helps people, it's not a publicity ploy. It's because he really cares."

"I want to be remembered as a guy that treated everyone the way I wanted to be treated," Casey says. "A guy that loved, a guy that was good to his teammates, and played hard every day. A guy that worked hard on and off the field, and got the most out of his abilities. A guy that had a couple of tools and refined the other tools and played the game hard every day. A man that treated everyone with respect and showed His love every day to everyone.

"I think sometimes the best testimony is the way you live your life and also the way you reach out to others. So I guess for me it's the way I show the love to everybody and hopefully God's love comes out...going to the everyday way you treat people—whether it is the clubhouse guy or teammates or an opposing player. I think that is the way God's love comes across."

The Heart of a Champion walks in integrity and kindness to all people:

What more can be said of Sean Casey's approach to life than what others have already said about him. His genuine personality is remarkable to his peers because these men are so used to seeing that which is counterfeit. So many athletes are surrounded by multitudes of people who want something from them—time, money, fame, or esteem through association—even from their peers. Casey wants nothing from those he comes in contact with but to leave a good deposit in their lives. He wants to treat people with kindness and respect—a simple thing, but so rare today. Because he has given respect and kindness, Casey has received that back, and his reputation continues to precede him.

What is the price of one's reputation? A good name can never really be bought, promoted, or forced. It is earned. Think of those you know who have a good name. What have they done to gain that reputation? The stark reality is that we have precious few opportunities to establish a good name. For once a reputation is built and circulated in our circles of influence, it is largely there to stay. What do people say about you when you are not around? What is your reputation and what is it based on? A good name is to be valued beyond any accomplishment or material standing. And people don't care how much you know until they know how much you care. They don't care what you have until they have your care. Think upon this: When your days here are done, how do you want to be remembered?

A good name is more desirable than great riches;
to be esteemed is better than silver or gold.

—Proverbs 22:1

PERSPECTIVE:

A champion sees good in the bad.

At some point in every player's career in baseball, adversity hits them. Injuries, slumps, booing crowds, trades, and errors—this is a game built on failure. What separates the best in the game from the rest is their ability to handle adversity and bounce back. Cincinnati Reds first baseman Sean Casey is one who saw adversity change his perspective both figuratively and literally. Known around the game as "the nicest man in baseball," Casey learned firsthand that bad things happen to nice guys and discovered that those bad things can turn out for good.

On the eve of the 1998 season, Casey was traded to the Reds from the Cleveland Indians. The 1995 NCAA batting champion at the University of Richmond tore up minor league pitching while making a rapid ascent through the Indians system, hitting .329, .331, and .380 in three seasons and becoming one of the top hitting prospects in all of baseball. He was highly coveted by a number of teams seeking to make a trade. The Reds won the sweepstakes. Three days following the trade, Casey was on the field for batting practice before a game, when an errant throw from a teammate struck him in the right eye. The accident resulted in four badly broken orbital bones. Surgeons performed a four-hour operation, in which they inserted five screws and a titanium plate around Casey's eye and attempted to repair double vision. Casey's future was in doubt.

"I went blind a few days in my right eye," Casey recalls. "I didn't know if I would ever play baseball again. I had permanent damage to my iris; to this day my pupil does not dilate like the other one. I did not know if I would be able to play again."

Lying in bed at Cincinnati's Good Samaritan Hospital, Casey pondered his future and looked for reasons to be thankful. "My faith in God really helped me through that because baseball really became a side note," Casey says. "I remember there were a lot of nights I would sit alone in my bed when all the visitors had gone and the nurses weren't there, and I kind of talked to God. And I realized that circumstances happen in your life and sometimes you don't know why they happen, and you're patient to make it through whatever He has in store for you.

"I believe that I was in that hospital room for a reason. It was okay that I was in that bed at that time hoping that one day I would be back out there playing, and if I wasn't then I would be happy doing something else. It offered me a lot of peace.

"There were a lot of times I lay in that bed and thought, *Thank You for the days I didn't play in the big leagues. Whatever You have in store for me is okay; there is nothing that I cannot handle.*"

Casey did make it back. His vision still blurred, he bounced from Triple A Indianapolis to Cincinnati during the first half of the 1998 season, until he slowly regained his vision in June and was back with the Reds to stay. Casey's comeback was complete in 1999, when he hit .332 with 25 home runs and 99 RBIs in his first full season. He followed that in 2000 with 20 home runs, 85 RBIs and a .315 average, and in 2001 he hit .310 with 89 RBIs. He made two all-star teams for his play on the field and was recognized for his character, receiving the Hutch Award in 1999 for spirit, courage, and integrity. During the process, his eyesight not only fully returned but even improved. An astigmatism he had in his right eye prior to the injury was suddenly no longer there. Casey was able to stop using a contact lens in that eye (he still uses one in his left eye) and was seeing clearly—one of the good things that came out of a very difficult event.

Life Lessons from Baseball

"When I first came back, I realized that baseball is really a game, and nothing is promised to you," Casey says. "What the Lord promises is love every day, and that baseball will only last so long. At twenty-four I thought my career might be over. Yet I think I was okay with that because I was fortunate to be in the big leagues at that point, and I realized that God has a plan for me and He is holding me and leading me into the direction He wants me to go.

"It put my life in perspective and made me take a few steps backward and realize how good God is. I realized that we really have to take one day at a time, that He offers us His Kingdom one day at a time. I was blessed to come back out on the field and play every day."

The Heart of a Champion knows that God works out every situation for good:

In all that Sean Casey went through, he never lost a positive perspective. Even in the most difficult moments of not knowing what the future might hold, he still believed there was purpose in the circumstances. He kept seeking what God wanted to do through his situation. He could never have imagined that at the end of the process, the eyesight in his right eye would be better than it had been since childhood. It was not even a thought that his trials would endear him to the Cincinnati fans even before he had played one game for his new team. He had no idea that his challenges gave him a platform to have an influence, as many watched him endure hardship without losing his joy. Nor did he realize the changes that would be made in his own perspective. For Casey, the result of his experience was all for the good.

When trials hit we often ask, "Why me?" "Why this?" or "Why now?" We wonder how God could allow something so difficult to hit us at such a time. Yet we must remember that God is not the author of evil and that we are subject to a fallen world. Still, God's promise is that He will use everything that affects us for our good and the good of others. It is so hard to believe that principle, especially when we enter a circumstance or season of trial and cannot see what is on the other side. This is where raw, uncluttered faith must abound—a radical trust that God is in control and is working it all for good. We must trust that something is taking place in a larger realm than we can see, beyond our circumstances. If we don't trust, we risk bitterness settling into our hearts. If we do trust, at some point we will be able to see the handiwork of God fashioning something great out of our hardship.

Our light and momentary troubles are achieving for us an eternal glory that far outweighs them all. So we fix our eyes not on what is seen, but on what is unseen. For what is seen is temporary, but what is unseen is eternal.

—2 Corinthians 4:17-18

Profile of CHARLES JOHNSON

"You have to want to catch every day, in the hot sun, with all that gear on and with balls hitting you. Catching is a position that you have to love. To me, it's fun . . . it comes from the heart."

TRUST:

A champion trusts the ultimate coach.

He has the hands of a surgeon or world-class musician. The palms are smooth, pink, and soft; the fingers long and straight; their movements graceful and nimble. Yet these are not hands that save lives or create masterpieces—these are the hands of baseball's record-setting catcher, Charles Johnson.

The same hands also used to clean house after school, wash dishes after dinner, and survive point-blank rounds of fastballs shot from a backyard pitching machine. All of these experiences played a role in the success of the multiple Gold Glove Award-winning backstop who holds the major league record for the most consecutive errorless games (172) and the most consecutive errorless chances (1,294) by a catcher.

How did Johnson, who has started for the Florida Marlins, Los Angeles Dodgers, Baltimore Orioles, Chicago White Sox, and Colorado Rockies, get to be so good behind the plate? The answer to that goes back twenty-plus years.

In his family's backyard in Fort Pierce, Florida, Charles Johnson Sr. decided one day that if his son really wanted to become a catcher, it was time to put that desire to the test. After all, Charles Jr. had come to him not long before and told him that an entire year spent playing left field in Little League had been too boring. He wanted a challenge; he wanted to catch. It was time to let the boy learn what he was in for and see if he could do it. So the father stood by his new pitching machine, ready to feed it baseballs. In front of him—just ten feet away—squatted nine-year-old Charles Jr. in full catcher's gear. His father fed a ball into the machine, which was aimed directly at the boy's heart, literally and figuratively. With a whirl, the baseball blasted out of the machine and sped toward Charles Jr. He was not quick enough. With a loud thud, the ball slammed against his chest protector.

Charles Jr.'s mother, Gloria, having watched the scene from the kitchen window of the Johnson's home, shouted for her husband to stop, as tears began to well in her eyes. "Why don't you leave him alone? You're going to kill him!" Charles Jr. remembers his mother yelling.

But Charles Sr. persisted, one ball after another. Each one drilled the boy in the chest. "It was the scariest moment of my life," admits Charles Sr., then the baseball coach at Westwood High School. "But I couldn't let him know it."

On ball number five, something that would change the future of Charles Johnson Jr. occurred: he caught the ball. "He started smiling," Charles Sr. says. "It was like a light went on. He realized, 'If I can catch the ball from 10 feet away, 60 feet is no problem. All fear left him.'"

Similar workouts in the yard continued thereafter, with Charles Sr. and his brother, Roy, both former college players, putting in hours of teaching. With the family's old toolshed as a backstop, the two men invested hours into Charles Jr., schooling him on footwork and framing pitches, and blocking balls in the dirt. Day after day Charles Sr. would fire fifty baseballs into the dirt in front of his squatting son. If the boy blocked at least forty-five of them, his father treated him to burgers at McDonald's.

"Some kids may have been doing other things, but my father had me in the backyard doing baseball things," says Charles. "Sometimes you don't understand. You say, 'Why am I doing this?' But there were times my father said, 'It's time to work a little bit,' and now I really appreciate that. . . . Sometimes I'd cry when balls hit me," says Charles. "But it showed me that I really wanted to catch."

"You have to want to catch every day, in the hot sun, with all that gear on and with balls hitting you. Catching is a position that you have to love. To me, it's fun . . . it comes from the heart."

Just as his father planned.

The Heart of a Champion is willing to trust the One who knows the future:

Charles Johnson Sr. understood a very important principle relating to his son's desire to play catcher. The elder Johnson knew that if his son was to ever make it at the position, he had to be free of the fear of being hit by the ball. If Charles Jr. overcame that fear at an early age, he would not struggle with it again. Because Charles Jr. trusted his father, he was willing to position himself ten feet away from a pitching machine firing balls at his chest. Johnson's trust in his father's method laid the foundation for him to become an all-star player.

The relationship between Charles Johnson and his father is a wonderful metaphor for our relationship with our Heavenly Father. God often puts us in a position that seems only ten feet in front of the barrel of a pitching machine. "How could You put me here?" we cry.

"Because I love you," He gently responds.

Putting us in that position reminds us that in handling it, we become better able to handle even greater things. It all comes down to trust. Charles Johnson Jr. didn't have the vision to see beyond the pitching machine to a pro career, but he trusted his father. You may not have the vision to see beyond circumstances that you currently face, but God does. That is why He has you there. The question is, can you simply trust Him?

Trust in the LORD with all your heart and lean not on your own understanding; in all your ways acknowledge him, and he will make your paths straight.

—Proverbs 3:5-6

COURAGE:

A champion does not fear the judgment of others.

When then eight-year-old Charles Johnson Jr. approached his father and announced, "I want to be a big league catcher," it not only surprised the boy's father, but it was an unusual idea. On the summer day of 1981 when Charles Jr., dressed in full catcher's gear, squatted in his backyard waiting to catch his first pitch, twenty-five of the twenty-six starting catchers in the major leagues were white. One was Hispanic. None were black.

The last time a big league team had started an African-American as an everyday catcher was in 1979, when Gary Alexander was behind the plate for the Cleveland Indians. But Johnson had a role model close by. His cousin, Terry McGriff, had played catcher for the Westwood High School team that Johnson's father coached, and he ended up signing with the Cincinnati Reds. Whenever the Westwood team played, Johnson would stand behind the backstop and study McGriff's every move. His study continued as McGriff rose through the Reds system and made it to big league level. His cousin became a huge inspiration for Johnson, who was convinced that he, too, could make it to the majors.

At thirteen, Charles participated in a baseball camp in Florida that attracted some of the better youth baseball talent from around the state. During one game a college player attempted to steal a base, and Charles gunned him down. It was then that Charles Sr. knew his son "was something special."

Life Lessons from Baseball

Charles went on to become a high school star at Westwood High. The Montreal Expos drafted him out of high school with the tenth pick in 1989, but he chose to attend the University of Miami-Florida instead, where he became an all-American and played on the U.S. Olympic team. In 1992 the expansion Florida Marlins made him the first player the franchise had ever drafted.

In 1995 the Marlins promoted Johnson to their starting catcher position for the beginning of the season. He became the first black man since Alexander to become a full-time catcher. In 1997 Johnson did not make a single error during the entire season, the first time a big league catcher had achieved that feat since 1946. In the fall of that year he helped the Marlins win the 1997 World Series. After several fine seasons, in 2000 Johnson became a bona fide star when he hit .304 with 31 home runs and 91 RBIs. By 2003 he had won four Gold Glove Awards for his defense and had been successful throwing out 60 percent of the few who attempted to steal on him during his career.

None of this fazed Johnson. Early on, his parents had given as much attention to preparing him for life as they had in preparing him to block balls in the dirt. Says his father, "What we stressed even more than baseball was being good and respectful around the house. Baseball was just a game. The person, that's the most important thing."

As a boy, Charles would hurry home from school to clean the house before his mother returned home from her job. He also washed dishes after dinner. Johnson felt it was the least he could do to support his parents and set an example for his three younger siblings. "My father and mother grew up having to pick oranges and tomatoes in the hot sun," he says. "How hard was cleaning compared to what they did? I was happy to do it."

He is still happy to do it. Whenever Johnson and his wife, Rhonda, who live in a Miami suburb not too far from his parents, make the drive north to visit for dinner, it is like old times again. Inevitably, Charles Sr. talks to his son about his footwork and catching mechanics. And when the meal is done, Charles Jr. heads back to the sink to handle the dirty dishes.

The Heart of a Champion is willing to conquer new territories:

It would have been much easier for Charles Johnson to stay in left field while pursuing his big league dream. After all, since the days that Jackie Robinson broke baseball's color barrier, there have been but a handful of African-American starting catchers in the major leagues. Yet Johnson, a very quiet and unassuming man, felt a sense of destiny to play the position. Having his cousin as an example certainly helped, but it undoubtedly also magnified the challenges. Throughout the past fifty years, most African-American catchers have been stereotyped as strong hitters who are weak defensively. Johnson knew the only way to break that label was to prove the contrary. He did so and became a star—all without losing his humility or forgetting those who helped him get there.

Courage is not necessarily best characterized by the portrayals of superheroes in movies and television—bloodied but still standing after polishing off the enemy. Rather, courage is knowing what is right and doing it anyway. Most often courage is accompanied by humility and restraint. The right path is often the most difficult one. Moral courage not only pushes us onto that path but it also restrains us in the pursuit of that end and dictates how we respond to recognition. Jesus knew that His path led to the Cross, and as difficult as the end was, He chose that path all the way to the end. In that pursuit, He remained restrained and humble, the perfect model of moral courage. The challenge for us is simple: when you know what is right, choose it, regardless of personal cost. The benefit will always outweigh the cost.

> *God did not give us a spirit of timidity, but*
> *a spirit of power, of love and of self-discipline.*
>
> —2 Timothy 1:7

Profile of RANDY JOHNSON

"A question you have to ask is, 'Do you feel complete?' I feel I am. I've been blessed with four kids, a beautiful wife, and a career that's taken off through God's blessings. Still, I know I'm going to make mistakes, so I spend a lot of time praying. That helps me stay strong in my commitment to Him and to doing what He wants me to do."

PERSPECTIVE:

A champion finds good in all things.

R andy Johnson can recall his first experience with organized baseball. When he was six years old, he attended a Little League tryout in his hometown of Livermore, California. "I went there by myself because my mom and dad both worked," he recalled. "There I was with a bunch of other kids feeling like a lost puppy dog. I didn't know where to go, whom to see. I got lost, started crying, and went home."

When his mom returned and saw her son upset, she took him back to the tryouts and got him on a team. "She knew I wanted to play," Johnson said. "And when I think about it, if she hadn't taken me back, I might not be where I am today."

Where he is today is firmly entrenched as the most dominating pitcher of this era with Cy Young Awards from both leagues. Hitters fear him.

Johnson never would have become so successful without the gentle nudge from his mother all those years ago. Nor would he have dominated the mound without the assistance of pitching great Nolan Ryan, who mentored Johnson in 1993 and changed him from a "thrower" to a refined pitcher.

However, the story of Johnson's rise came at the same time he experienced other changes. From 1992-94, Johnson was hit by a twenty-four month emotional meteor shower of death, marriage, birth, and spiritual birth.

In 1992 Randy's father, Bud, suffered an aortic aneurysm while Randy was flying home to spend Christmas with his parents. By the time Randy made it to the hospital, his father had died. He laid his head on his father's chest, wept, and cried out, "Why'd you have to go now? It's not time."

He was so crushed that he told his mother, Carol, "I don't know if I want to pitch anymore. I'm thinking of quitting." Carol advised him to stick with it, and Randy eventually agreed. Searching for meaning, he also became a Christian and drew a cross and the word *DAD* on the palm of his glove. He glanced at the markings whenever he needed strength on the mound.

"I became a Christian when my father died," Johnson says of his turnaround. "I had believed in God, but He wasn't part of my daily life. When my dad died, it was hard for me to accept that he was gone. I had a lot of questions; it was very difficult for me to get through it. But God really helped. He gave me strength.

"Yes, changing my mechanics was a key, but that's just a small part of it. My heart got bigger. Determination can take you a long way. After my dad died, I was convinced I could get through anything. I don't use the word *pressure* anymore. That's for what he went through—life or death. I use the word *challenge*. And I'll never again say, 'I can't handle it.' I just dig down deeper."

His marriage and the birth of his daughter, Samantha, became other events that affected him deeply. Johnson's heart enlarged.

"A question you have to ask is, 'Do you feel complete?' I feel I am. I've been blessed with four kids, a beautiful wife, and a career that's taken off through God's blessings. Still, I know I'm going to make mistakes, so I spend a lot of time praying. That helps me stay strong in my commitment to Him and to doing what He wants me to do.

"I mean, if you look at it, I was barely a .500 pitcher before my dad died, and I got married and had a baby," he exclaims. "My wife and baby have brought me down to earth. I'm not as selfish as I used to be. Win or lose, I always have them to come home to."

Randy Johnson understands that while the various seasons of his life have brought both good and bad, everything has been a means to strengthen his relationship with God.

"I'm working for Him out there, giving my best effort," Johnson says. "God's given me the ability, and I don't want to waste it. That's why I work extremely hard. I don't want to look back and say I wasted the gifts God gave me."

The Heart of a Champion understands that God's plan is perfect:

In 1993 Randy Johnson was a hard-throwing, 6-foot-10-inch, left-handed pitcher on the verge of becoming a footnote in baseball history. A change of heart revolutionized his career and life. Johnson was confused about his pitching, confused about life, and seeking answers. He found them when he found God, but it took hardship to get there. The death of his father was devastating, but it was also the catalyst to finding faith and growing personally and as a pitcher.

Trials are difficult. But through them, God has a purpose beyond what we can see. What trouble or trial are you facing in your life? What do you trust God to bring out of it? Trust Him in your trials. Nothing you face has caught Him by surprise. He sees it all and will use it all for a greater purpose. This may very well be the beginning of a life-changing experience for you.

We know that in all things God works for
the good of those who love him, who have
been called according to his purpose.

—Romans 8:28

Profile of TODD JONES

*"I want to help the
Tigers, and if I can
help the Tigers by
being traded,
that's fine."*

HUMILITY:

A champion puts others first.

From 1997 to 2001, Todd Jones was one of baseball's top closers. Yet at the height of an effective five-run stretch, in which only five other pitchers saved more than his 184 games, Jones forgot that baseball is supposed to be a coldhearted business.

Jones, who pitched in his first all-star game in 2000, was entering into the final year of his contract with the Detroit Tigers the following season. When asked by the press throughout the season about his stance for the coming off-season regarding a new contract, Jones stunned them with his response. The veteran pitcher told media members that even though he was coming off the best seasons of his career, he would *not* seek an exorbitant salary or a no-trade clause if Detroit offered him a contract extension. He further astonished the press by telling them that as long as he remained a Tiger in 2001, he would work to groom his eventual successor, Matt Anderson.

"It's my job, if I move on, to have a seamless transition from me to him," Jones said at the time of his relationship with Anderson. "If he doesn't do his job, then I've failed. I want to help the Tigers, and if I can help the Tigers by being traded, that's fine."

Jones did return to the Tigers for the final year of his contract in 2001, knowing he would likely be traded before September. At the end of July, as playoff contenders were looking for pitching help, the Tigers shipped Jones to the Minnesota Twins, who needed a bull-pen boost. When he was informed of the news of the deal,

Jones responded with the same humility and graciousness that he had all along.

"It was an honor to be a Tiger and to have thrown the last pitch at Tiger Stadium," he said at the time. "This team and this city have touched my heart, but the time has come to move on; and I'm excited, at the age of thirty-three, to get a shot at the postseason with Minnesota."

Jones tied for the American League lead in saves in 2000 with 42, setting a Tigers single-season record. During his career in Detroit, he totaled 142 saves, second in club history. But midway through the 2001 season, the team began the transition of moving Anderson into the closer's role. Even after the trade to Minnesota, Jones still felt a sense of responsibility to the Tigers.

"Early in the year, I felt like I had let the whole city down, but now I know that isn't true," he said. "Matty was ready to be the closer. Maybe I can come back next year in a setup role. I just wish I could have brought the Tigers a little more in the deal."

The Heart of a Champion values the success of others:

Todd Jones' response to his situation with the Tigers is quite rare. His concerns for his own future seemed to be secondary to his sense of commitment and responsibility to the Detroit franchise. To put his attention on preparing his successor and on how he would best benefit the team he would be departing is the attitude many athletes carried in years past, but it is uncommon today. Those who know the pitcher say such feelings are completely genuine and typical of his character.

Such loyalty seems scarce today, as the messages around us constantly urge us to put ourselves first and everything else behind. But this is a dangerous game. When we look after our own interests above all else, we end up placing self on the throne of our lives. Narcissism follows, and then ultimately self-destruction. We were not created to be self-centered. We were created to be others-centered. God alone must fill the throne of our heart, and He will not share that throne with any other being or thing. When He occupies that throne, His nature moves us to give of ourselves to others and to decrease so that others may increase. In this action there is true fulfillment and joy.

All of you, clothe yourselves with humility toward one another, because, "God opposes the proud but gives grace to the humble." Humble yourselves, therefore, under God's mighty hand, that he may lift you up in due time.

—1 Peter 5:5-6

Profile of JEFF KING

"I really didn't want to leave. I liked Pittsburgh, and my family's home was there. Maybe I could find a better situation as a free agent, but why risk it when I was perfectly happy where I was?"

HUMILITY:

Champions do not over-estimate their importance.

J eff King, a highly coveted slugger from the University of Arkansas, was the first overall pick in the 1986 amateur baseball draft. He made his way through the Pittsburgh Pirates organization, constantly striving to succeed in the face of high expectations.

He made it permanently in 1989, and by 1993 he had become one of the game's top run-producing third basemen. After the 1994 season, King was eligible for free agency and appeared ready to move to a contending team for more money. After all, playing for the cost-conscious, small-market Pirates wasn't where he would earn the most money or get a chance to play for a World Series contender.

But at the height of his prime market value, while most other major league teams were waiting to make him a lucrative financial offer, King made an unusual decision. He decided he wanted to be loyal to the team that had been loyal to him. He wanted to stay in Pittsburgh. So he put his character and priorities ahead of a paycheck and negotiated a one-year deal that called for an 11 percent *pay cut!*

"I really didn't want to leave," King says. "I liked Pittsburgh, and my family's home was there. Maybe I could find a better situation as a free agent, but why risk it when I was perfectly happy where I was?"

In putting personal contentment first, King became an anomaly in the world of sports—a successful player who turned down more money and took a reduced salary to stay with the team that had nurtured his career.

Five years later the character King demonstrated would once again show through, when he told the Kansas City Royals he would gladly pass on a $3 million-per-year contract.

King was in the midst of a $4 million-per-year contract with the Royals following his trade from Pittsburgh in 1997. It was May, the season was still fresh, and King was playing well and adding to career numbers that showed over 150 home runs and 700 RBIs in ten years. And then he simply walked away.

King realized he didn't have a desire to play baseball anymore. He couldn't go back out on the field and make it look like he wanted to be there. His heart was back on his ranch in Montana with his wife, Laura, and their children. So he retired. In doing so, he gave up the $3 million left on his contract and his remaining professional goals. Unlike some who might have coasted through the season to collect paychecks, King felt he didn't deserve money he wasn't earning. He simply wanted a different life in Montana with his family. So Jeff King walked away, understanding that some things are more important than money.

The Heart of a Champion knows that true value is not found in material things:

Jeff King's actions are unique and even astonishing in his era. When, in recent memory, can you recall an athlete, an entertainer, or a corporate head negotiating a pay cut to stay with their team or company? How about passing up millions from another team or company to stay put when the contract was up? Why would Jeff King do this? He recognized that some things really are more important than money. For King, peace of mind, family contentment, and individual joy were tantamount to financial reward. Jeff

Life Lessons from Baseball

King realized he had a great situation and didn't need anything more to be content.

As the story goes, when asked the question, "How much does it take to make a man truly happy?" billionaire businessman John D. Rockefeller replied, "Just a little bit more." Whether or not the event actually happened, it serves as a representation of our culture: "I'm not fulfilled yet, but I will be if I can just have a little more _____." You can fill in the blank yourself—more money, more power, more prestige, more house, more car, and so on. This perspective leads us on a never-ending search for just a little bit more. The trap is that we are never truly satisfied with what we have, and no matter how high we raise the bar, we will always have to reach higher to find happiness—or so we think. Yet true fulfillment is found in the simple things in life. Money can buy you a bed, but not sleep; a house, but not a home. Don't be caught in the trap of always seeking "a little bit more." A thankful heart will lead to a peace and a joy that material things cannot bring. True peace and joy can be found only in the presence of a loving God.

*Keep your lives free from the love of money and be
content with what you have, because God has said,
"Never will I leave you; never will I forsake you."
So we say with confidence, "The Lord is my helper;
I will not be afraid. What can man do to me?"*

—Hebrews 13:5-6

Profile of CHAD KREUTER

"All the different people that called while I was in ICU or rehabbing, saying that they were praying for me—it meant a lot and obviously God heard those prayers because what happened in surgery was very miraculous."

PERSEVERANCE:

A champion never gives up.

D o you believe in miracles? Chad Kreuter does. This major league catcher came back to baseball in 1997, less than a year after a devastating shoulder injury nearly ended his career. More than that, doctors thought Kreuter might never regain use of his left arm for everyday functions—even after a five-hour operation in which $40,000 worth of rods and screws were used to repair his shoulder. But Kreuter disregarded the doctors' prognosis, disobeyed their rehab rules, leaned on his faith, and devised a creative program for a miraculous recovery.

"They originally told me that I'd never play again because of the injury—let alone comb my hair, brush my teeth, or function normally," Kreuter says. "After them telling me that, I feel really blessed to be able to do all of the above."

The ordeal began on July 19, 1996. The play did not initially appear particularly violent. As the 6-foot-2-inch, 200-pound Kreuter, then of the Chicago White Sox, reached for a short hop throw from right field, Kansas City Royals 6-foot-2-inch, 196-pound, freight train of an outfielder, Johnny Damon, plowed into Kreuter's outstretched shoulder at an awkward angle.

"I was in a very vulnerable position," says Kreuter. "All the angles were wrong in the sense that it completely blew my shoulder out. Instead of getting hit square, I was hit at the angle that it not only separated my shoulder, it completely shattered it."

The diagnosis was "severe separation and multiple fractures," but the shoulder was shattered like glass, with bits and pieces sprayed all over. Doctors likened it to an injury motorcyclists incur when they crash into trees or light poles at a high rate of speed. The pain was nearly unbearable.

"It felt like somebody was holding me down," Kreuter says. "It felt like my left shoulder was attached to my right shoulder. It felt like somebody had a knife in my shoulder somewhere in the middle of my back, and I was laying on it. I knew something was wrong."

"In 20 years of baseball, it's one of the most dramatic fractures and injuries I've ever seen," says Lewis Yocum, one of the two surgeons who operated. "He was Humpty Dumpty."

While the shoulder injury threatened Kreuter's career, undetected internal bleeding threatened his life. Kreuter was scheduled to have shoulder surgery in Los Angeles four days after the collision. But he fainted in his hotel shower the day before the operation, scaring his wife, Kelly, who found him passed out.

"He was convulsing, and his eyes were rolled in his head," says Kelly, who called 911. Paramedics responded immediately, transporting Kreuter to a nearby hospital within minutes. The speedy reaction saved Kreuter's life. But then, so did passing out in the shower.

"They told me that if I had gone into surgery the next day with that kind of blood loss, I might have flat-lined," Kreuter says. He spent the next five days in intensive care until he recovered enough to have the operation.

Yocum and fellow surgeon Robert Chandler reconstructed the shoulder, piecing bone fragments together like a jigsaw puzzle. They anchored the joint with seven one-inch screws and two steel plates.

Still, Kreuter was determined to come back. He disregarded the doctors' orders and pushed himself to his limits and beyond. The doctors told him to wear a sling. He never did. They told him to keep his arm still for a month. He was in the pool exercising within two days. They told him to stick to passive stretching, with someone else lifting his arm while he did nothing. Kreuter convinced a physical therapist to perform exercises his doctors would have ruled out.

"I understand from the doctors' point of view that people have come after them with lawsuits, and they can't be too aggressive," Kreuter says. "But I said if I was ever gonna play major league baseball again, I had to take things into my own hands. I put them in the Lord's hands and let Him guide me. I knew my body would tell me what I can and can't do as I went along."

Less than a year later, Kreuter was back behind the plate. Chad and Kelly, who are Christians, gave God ultimate credit for Chad's recovery.

"All the different people that called while I was in ICU or rehabbing, saying that they were praying for me—it meant a lot, and obviously God heard those prayers," says Chad, "because what happened in surgery was very miraculous. The doctor's own words were, 'Muscles moved around, bones moved around very miraculously.' We know Christ played a huge role in this."

The Heart of a Champion refuses to give up, no matter the odds:

Chad Kreuter's story is a clear example of a man possessing strong internal fortitude and an abundance of faith. He was not willing to be satisfied with the prognosis of the doctors, when he felt God was telling him something different. Because of this, he refused to pack everything up and go home, happy with merely being able to brush his teeth again. He wanted something more and believed that was in God's plan, so he went after it.

So often the world around us tells us what we are not and what we can't do. Rarely does any part of the world tell us what we are and what we can do. The world is full of naysayers, skeptics, and critics. But God wants to tell you what you are and what you can do through His empowerment. When everything around you says you can't, go to God and inquire of Him. Listen for His response. Then, whatever He tells you to do—do it with all your heart, soul, and strength. The results, oftentimes, will be far beyond what you or anyone else ever could have imagined—sometimes even miraculous.

I can do everything through him who gives me strength.

—Philippians 4:13

Profile of PAUL LO DUCA

"I know I'm blessed that God gave me the talent to do what I do and gave this opportunity to do what I've done, and I'm a firm believer that none of this would happen without the Man above."

PERSEVERANCE:

A champion never quits.

Paul Lo Duca shocked the baseball world in 2001, coming from relative oblivion to post a historic season. The Los Angeles Dodgers catcher hit .320, with 25 home runs and 90 RBIs, and struck out just 30 times in 460 official at bats—the lowest strikeout total for any player hitting 25 or more homers since 1956. He also threw out 39 percent of the runners that tried to steal against him and established himself as a budding all-star.

It was an amazing entrance to the big leagues and didn't happen until Lo Duca had turned twenty-nine and endured eight seasons in the minor leagues, with only 76 games at the big league level scattered here and there, and only limited playing time as a backup. But when Lo Duca was finally given his chance, he responded and quickly became a fan favorite.

After setting records for single-season batting average (.446) and hits (129) during his one year at Arizona State University, Lo Duca was drafted in the twenty-fifth round by the Dodgers in 1993. He never hit less than .305 in a full season, but he couldn't convince Dodgers management that he was a major leaguer. The shortcomings included his size—he's closer to 5 feet 8 inches than his listed height of 5 feet 10 inches—and he won't hit for power; he's only fair defensively.

Lo Duca determined not to become bitter. Instead, he focused on becoming better. He worked diligently with Mike Scioscia, who was a roving catching instructor in the L.A. organization. Scioscia challenged Lo Duca on his mental approach and how to call a game and then he helped him with his catching and throwing mechanics. It all took.

Still, there were roadblocks. Ahead of Lo Duca in L.A. at the time was future Hall of Famer Mike Piazza. Piazza was traded in 1998, but in exchange the Dodgers received Gold Glover Charles Johnson. After Johnson came all-star Todd Hundley and then prized prospect Angel Pena. Stuck behind Pena, and sitting on the bench to open the 2000 season, Lo Duca hit a low point. Thinking he had no future, he considered getting out of baseball. But Lo Duca knew that his late mother would not have wanted him to quit. His wife, Sonja, and his father, Paul Sr., reinforced the message. Lo Duca resolved that once he got the chance to play, there would be no getting him out of the lineup. He tore up the Pacific Coast League, hitting .351 that year, and as he went into spring training to start the 2001 season, Dodgers Manager Jim Tracy told him he was the team's number-one catcher until further notice. Lo Duca got off to a hot start, including pounding 6 hits in a game against Colorado, and he was on his way.

"People identify with Paul because they know it didn't come easily for him," Tracy said. "He more than paid his dues with all that time in the minors, and the success he had is something he earned."

He is still earning his way. Buoyed by an intense competitive desire, Lo Duca is always working at the game—extra hitting, extra weightlifting, and extra footwork. He is a bundle of enthusiasm, tireless in his dedication to improve and give his all.

"I'm a firm believer for, two-and-a-half, three hours, however long the game is, it's not hard to run your hardest ninety feet or to run out to your position nine times a day," Lo Duca says. "I'm the kind of guy that goes 110 percent every play, and I want to be known as that. I don't want to be known as the guy that when a guy drops a fly ball, I'm standing at first base. I want to be the guy that's sliding into second. I want to be the guy that's hustling and smart. I'm not blessed with the best skills, but I want to be the guy that has the most heart and is going to give you all that I've got.

Life Lessons from Baseball

"I play the game like you played in your backyard when you were a little kid or when you played whiffle ball. I get a little excited out there, and I jump around, but that's just part of me having fun, and that's the way I want to play.

"I think everybody, when they become a professional baseball player, they set a timetable on when they want to get to the big leagues. I think my timetable was to get there in three or four years. Well, it just didn't happen for me. I got stuck behind some pretty good players. It just wasn't meant to be for me here at the time. I think it might have been a blessing in disguise. I thought I could have been up here when I was twenty-four . . . twenty-five, and I don't know if I would have been able to handle it and been able to be as humble as I am because of the adversity I did go through. Me being a little bit older made me mature a lot more.

"I know I'm blessed that God gave me the talent to do what I do and gave me this opportunity to do what I've done and I'm a firm believer that none of this would happen without the Man above."

The Heart of a Champion never gives up on the dream God has given:

Paul Lo Duca had many opportunities to quit baseball. For eight straight years, when he learned that he had been assigned to a minor league team, he had a choice to persevere or quit. Lo Duca chose to persevere and continue to follow his dream. Even though he continued to have all-stars in front of him, even though he never seemed to get his chance, he pressed on. Lo Duca chose not to focus on the things he couldn't change, but rather, focused on the things he could change. He worked to become the best he could become and left the other things up to God.

It is so easy for us to throw a pity party when things don't go our way. We look at all of the obstacles in our way and ask God why He hasn't made things easier for us. We ask Him to change the circumstances. Yet God often wants to use the circumstances to speak to us about us. Just as Paul Lo Duca became determined to get better, we should use our times of frustration to ask God what He wants to change about "me." Our gifts will always make a way for us, but often we are not ready for the opportunity that is to come because we have not given God the freedom to work in us to prepare us for the moment. Don't get bitter—get better. At the same time you ask God to change your circumstance, also ask Him to change you.

One thing I do: Forgetting what is behind and straining toward what is ahead, I press on toward the goal to win the prize for which God has called me heavenward in Christ Jesus.

—Philippians 3:13-14

THANKFULNESS:

Champions never forget those who helped them.

While Paul Lo Duca's journey to the major leagues is one of perseverance, it is also a testament to the effort and love of a caring mother. For many big leaguers, it was a father who inspired them, but for Paul it was his mother, Luci, who first instilled in him a love for the game and a commitment to hard work.

Because of Luci, Paul has worked overtime to develop his baseball skills ever since he was a young boy. His mother would put on oversized sunglasses to protect her eyes and pitch pinto beans to Paul in the backyard of the family's Phoenix, Arizona, home. The theory was that if Paul could hit the tiny beans, his hand-eye coordination would be sharpened, and the skills necessary for hitting a much larger baseball would come more easily.

Luci was Paul's greatest encourager when it came to his baseball career. More than pitching beans in the backyard, she also constantly pitched Paul on the belief that he could make it in the big leagues no matter how difficult the road looked. It is from Luci that Paul inherited his firm resolve to never give up.

"My mother was a huge part of my life," says Lo Duca. "My dad always was a real hard worker and held a couple jobs, so it was me and my mother a lot when I was a teenager and she was a baseball purist. She was my biggest supporter in the whole world. She took me to all my games, she took me to the batting cages . . . the only regret I have in my life is that she wasn't able to see me play at this level, because she's the one that instilled for me to keep going and not to give up."

Luci died of ovarian cancer in 1996, at age fifty-three, nearly two years before Paul reached the majors for the first time. Still, even after her death, her inspiration motivated Paul to keep pressing on when he felt like quitting.

At no time was that more evident than in 2000 when Lo Duca, stuck behind other Dodgers catchers and seemingly destined to spend his ninth year in the minor leagues, considered hanging up his cleats. Those thoughts were quickly squashed by remembering what his mother had told him in 1996 when he visited her in the hospital, just days before she died. Paul had been invited to play in the Arizona Fall League where top prospects are pitted against one another. Instead of playing, he had planned to take several weeks off to be with his family following his mother's death. Luci would have no such action. "I want you to come to the funeral, then I want you to play the next day," he says she told him. "This is your biggest break. This is the one that will get you to the big leagues." A few days later Lo Duca attended services for his mother, and the following day he caught for nine innings.

"The last thing I wanted to do was play ball, but I did it for her," he says.

In Luci's memory, when Paul steps onto the field before the start of every game, he is a walking, talking tribute to the woman who made it possible for him to be there.

"I put her initials in the dirt before every game with a cross, and I put her name on almost all my equipment," says Lo Duca. "It's just something to know that she's with me and just to honor her and know she's still part of me."

The Heart of a Champion remembers those who have helped along the way:

Paul Lo Duca will never forget the sacrifices his mother made to see him have a chance at a successful baseball career. He knows that if it were not for his mom, he would not be a major leaguer. Imagine her selfless dedication in pitching pinto beans to her son in the family's backyard. In honoring her, he has chosen to remember what she gave up for him and what she built into his life.

When we look back over the course of our lives, there are so many others who have sacrificed or helped us to move down the road of our experience. Yet it seems we rarely take time to honor them and their expressions of confidence, faith, and love toward us. How do you honor those who have inspired you? Jesus told us that when we partake of communion, we are to remember Him. Each time we will be reminded of the sacrifice He willingly made for us—the expression of love. Remember Him. Honor Him. And honor those who have been used along the way as an expression of His love toward you in helping or inspiring you in your journey.

> *The Lord Jesus, on the night he was betrayed,*
> *took bread, and when he had given thanks,*
> *he broke it and said, "This is my body, which*
> *is for you; do this in remembrance of me." In the*
> *same way, after supper he took the cup, saying,*
> *"This cup is the new covenant in my blood; do this,*
> *whenever you drink it, in remembrance of me."*
>
> —1 Corinthians 11:23-25

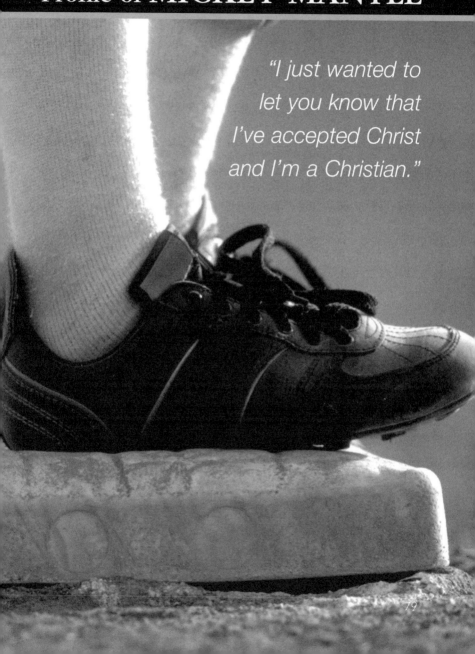

"I just wanted to let you know that I've accepted Christ and I'm a Christian."

FAITH:

A champion finds truth.

Mickey Charles Mantle was a hero to two generations. He was—for a time—bigger than the game itself. He still remains, to some, the epitome of baseball. A farm boy from Commerce, Oklahoma, Mantle came to the New York Yankees as an innocent teenager with boyish naiveté and left a national hero. Supremely gifted, he was a switch-hitter who possessed frightening power from either side of the plate and speed on the base paths. In the field he displayed a strong arm, cat-like reactions, and an uncanny knack for reading the ball.

Mantle could hit a ball farther than anyone else in the game. Nicknamed "The Commerce Comet," he was labeled by fans and experts alike as the greatest player who ever lived. Through world championships and pennant races, the bigger the game, the more Mantle rose to the occasion. The World Series record book is nearly an abridged Mantle autobiography. In New York he became a bona fide matinee idol on the biggest of all stages. He was baseball's golden boy; the real "Natural," with 536 career home runs and a bevy of records—all lessened by a succession of catastrophic leg injuries. Only God knows what many have pondered, "What might have been?"

Yet on the inside, the road of adversity punctuated by a series of bad choices were insidiously taking their toll on this "hero." We were later to find out what we had surmised all along. This man among men was still just a kid at heart. The folly of youth began to deteriorate the body and depress the soul.

In the blink of an eye, the valiant hero was nearly gone. Wracked with cancer, he was down to his last at bat. Yet it was the Mick's opportunity for a save. An old teammate who helped Mantle capture many a World Series crown came through with one last assist.

Former Yankee second baseman Bobby Richardson walked into Mickey's hospital room as the bottom of the ninth began. "His mind was crystal clear. He said, 'Bobby, it's so good to see ya.' And I said, 'Mickey, I love ya, and I just want you to spend eternity with me,'— we had talked about the Lord many times before—and he said, 'That's what I wanted to tell ya. I just wanted to let you know that I've accepted Christ and I'm a Christian.'

"I said, 'Mickey, that's wonderful! Let's just go over it to make sure.' And I just went over God's plan of salvation in a simple way that God loved us and had a plan and a purpose for our lives and sent the Lord Jesus Christ to shed His precious blood, and promised in His Word that if he would repent of his sin and receive the Lord Jesus, he might not only have everlasting life, but the joy of letting Him live His life in him. And he said, 'And that's just what I've done.'

"Then my wife, Betsy, knelt down by him and held his hand. Then she asked Mickey the question, 'Mickey, if God were here today, and He would ask you the question, "Why should I let you into My Heaven?", what would you say?'

"And his first response was, 'We're talking about God?' And she said, 'That's right, Mickey, we are.' And he quoted the verse John 3:16, 'For God so loved the world, that He gave His only begotten Son, that whosoever believeth in Him should not perish, but have everlasting life.'

"I don't know whether it was in the quietness of the moment with the Holy Spirit that he made a decision, or whether there were others that prompted him, but I do know that he made a decision for Christ, and that he had a peace there at the end. I was just absolutely thrilled! Not because it was Mickey Mantle, but because it was a close friend who would spend eternity with Christ."

Inspired by his new faith, the hero who had slipped from his pedestal decided to take one last cut. It was the biggest hit of his life. Mantle faced a nation of admirers and told them he had never been a role model. "Don't be like me," he said, "God gave me so much, and I wasted it."

Following his death, Mantle's story of faith came out. Everyone heard why he had changed in his final days. In one brief moment in dying, Mantle gave more to the world than he had in a lifetime as an icon.

The Heart of a Champion accepts the sacrificial love of Christ:

Mickey Mantle's final press conference was undoubtedly also his finest moment. It was a time in which Mantle became a true hero. Not for his strength to hit a ball, his speed to run the bases, or the grace with which he chased down fly balls. Rather, for his strength of character, his quickness to speak the truth, and the grace, humility, faith, and sacrifice he exhibited during his final moment in the sun. He faced an adoring world and sent a clear and simple message—*Don't follow me anymore; follow the One I've now chosen to follow.*

Life brings challenges to us all. Each of us has experienced being on a pedestal of sorts one moment and being removed the next. It is true that our lives are like a mist—here one day and gone into eternity the next. Because of this fact, and because there are so many aspects of our human experience that are out of our control, we must know the Savior. Our lives cannot be built upon our own accomplishments, good works, or the things we strive to attain. Our lives must be built on the foundation of the saving grace of Jesus Christ. Without it we are hopelessly lost both for time and eternity. Have you made the same decision Mickey Mantle chose to make in those hours when he surveyed the breadth of his life? If not, do so today. Choose life. Accept the love and sacrifice of Christ, and follow the One whom Mickey chose to follow. Then you, too, may have the peace Mantle had, and the same assurance of what lies ahead.

To all who received him, to those who believed in his name, he gave the right to become children of God— children born not of natural descent, nor of human decision or a husband's will, but born of God.

—John 1:12-13

"My players are like my children. I tell my people that if my children had never picked up a Bible; and they somehow ran across one later in life, and they read about Jesus, then I hope they would say, 'that reminds me of my dad.'"

RESPECT:

Champions treat their peers as true equals.

With constant scrutiny from fans and media, the pressure on major league players to perform creates an atmosphere that is sometimes explosive. The task of keeping players calm and focused falls on the manager. As a result, today's manager is part strategist, part cheerleader, part psychologist, and part father figure—all the while his job can be found hanging in the balance with each decision and game. Few balance it all better than Jerry Manuel, who has taken a relational approach to leading his men. His is a philosophy born of personal convictions.

"I've always believed that if you're going to lead anybody, you need to establish a relationship with them before you give them rules," says Manuel. "I've always said that rules without a relationship equal rebellion.

"They need to know who I am and where I'm coming from. That's important to establish early in a relationship, so that's basically the guideline that I follow. I let them know who I am and what I believe in—and when they come to my office, what to expect. But yet at the same time, I want them to have the freedom to be themselves more than anything else. Not the freedom to be who I want them to be but who they feel they need to be."

Manuel's ways have worked with his players, who respect and admire their manager and perform well for him. Most say they sense the freedom he has given them to grow as athletes and as individuals, along with his never-ending support. The combination has created an atmosphere of mutual respect.

"When he speaks to others, he doesn't have to go and say the four-letter words, he doesn't curse," says Manuel's longtime former pitching coach Nardi Contreras. "Does he get mad? Does he get upset? Yes, but all in love and in making sure that he gets ideas across—to play hard and play to win because our profession is to win. . . . Still, you know he cares about these people's hearts."

"To be in a clubhouse or be on a team knowing that you've got a manager that knows who you are, and knows what you believe in, and understands and supports it is huge," says infielder Tony Graffanino, who played under Manuel with the Chicago White Sox. "I've been in other clubhouses where it's not like that, with the freedoms that we're given here; the acceptance . . . knowing that I can just walk in his office and either talk about baseball or say, 'Hey, I've got something I need to talk to you about'; and it goes from him being my manager to him being my Christian brother. That makes it a lot easier."

Manuel has drilled into his players the virtues of a tireless work ethic, and a relentless, never-give-up style of play. His teams bunt, hit and run, steal, sacrifice, and get dirty. The words he has used to define their style are aggressive, fearless, liberated, having a vision for winning, and confrontational. From the very beginning of his tenure in the Windy City, Manuel gained the label as "The Great Communicator."

"One of the best communicators I've ever seen," says longtime White Sox coach Joe Nossek, "and I've been with fifteen managers."

"My players are like my children," says Manuel. "I tell my people that if my children had never picked up a Bible; and they somehow ran across one later in life, and they read about Jesus, then I hope they would say 'that reminds me of my dad.'"

The Heart of a Champion respects all people as unique individuals with purpose:

Jerry Manuel demonstrates a unique approach to leadership. Rather than the dictatorial attitude taken by many sports coaches, Manuel has placed relationship first. This takes humility and compassion. While many coaches motivate out of fear or reprisal, it is the rare few who inspire. Manuel inspires through his visionary leadership and by demonstrating that he truly cares about his players.

It is said that *people don't care how much you know until they know how much you care.* Jerry Manuel understands this principle. So does Jesus Christ. Has there ever been another to walk the face of the earth who knew as much as Jesus? Yet, with all of the wisdom of the Godhead, His life here would best be characterized by the frequency with which He made it a priority to first demonstrate His compassion, and then to teach out of the established relationship. Because He showed how much He cared for them, the people cared about His message. Is it the same with you? With those in your circle of influence, are you first instructional or relational? Show others respect and compassion, and you will open up a line of communication that will become very fruitful.

You are all sons of God through faith in Christ Jesus,
for all of you who were baptized into Christ have
clothed yourselves with Christ. There is neither
Jew nor Greek, slave nor free, male nor female,
for you are all one in Christ Jesus.

—Galatians 3:26-28

WISDOM:

A champion seeks wisdom.

J erry Manuel felt that he was fully prepared to manage in the major leagues when he took over the reins of the Chicago White Sox in 1998. As both a player and coach, Manuel had learned from some of the game's best managers—Felipe Alou of the Montreal Expos and Jim Leyland of the Florida Marlins. From them he learned not only how to manage with a focus on relationships but also how to read the players. Before batting practice on game days, Manuel is in deep thought. He walks to short center field, behind second base, and watches his player take batting practice, looking for intangibles.

"When batting practice comes up, I really don't like to be bothered," he says. "I'm studying the hitters to see who is swinging the bat well. That's why I watch so closely. If you have a feel, you've got to go with it."

"Jerry manages by the gut," says former White Sox general manager, Ron Schueler. "He does a lot of work on matchups, but then he says, 'I just got a gut feeling.'"

But that gut feeling does not come without intense study of game situations, and perhaps even more, an intense devotion to learning about people. The rural Georgia native is the epitome of calm. He is a philosopher in uniform, a fountain of wisdom. He is a Christian who is neither self-righteous nor rigid, but rather one possessing a dry and witty sense of humor and a fatherly appeal. He is a deep thinker who has studied the teachings of Martin Luther King and Mohandas Gandhi on subjects ranging from fasting to self-sac-rifice, all of which have profoundly shaped his character.

"I read those people to give me a better perspective on life," Manuel says. "And again, when I'm reading or when I'm studying a different man, I'm looking at him, thinking, *What can I gain from him to share with the men that I believe in?* And to me there were no greater *men* than Gandhi and Martin Luther King—that's just my opinion. But ultimately everything that they got, they got from Jesus Christ. So, why not really go to the Source, and study the Source, and then try to pass that on to the men that you're trying to not only have follow you but then sometime in their life become leaders as well."

Manuel had studied great leaders for years, and embraced their philosophies, yet still felt as if something was missing from his life. He found it one day in 1983, while he attended a Bible study with players from the Chicago Cubs, with whom he was in camp at the time. One of the participants was a catcher Manuel did not know. He had been cut from the team that day, but appeared to Manuel to be at perfect peace, even happy with the news, saying, "Now I can find out what God has in store for me. This is great."

Manuel stared at him in disbelief. "I knew he had something I wanted to have," he says. "The circumstances didn't move him. His belief is what he held on to. He was immovable."

After a few months of exploring, Manuel became a Christian and found a new purpose and dream that would sustain him through an array of jobs as a scout, instructor, minor league manager, and big league coach—all in preparation for the day when Schueler came calling on him for the White Sox job. The same purpose and dream sustain him today.

"Any time that I'm struggling or pressing or stressing—and all those things still happen to me regardless of what I believe in—then I have to go back and say, 'What would God do?' Or, 'Where is His kingdom? Where is His domain in this?' 'Where is His righteousness in this?' Then I find myself kind of getting above my situation."

The Heart of a Champion pursues wisdom and follows its path:

Jerry Manuel is a student of great philosophers. He has become well-versed in tenets of great leadership and relationship. He continues to study on a daily basis, always learning and gleaning from the wisdom of more experienced men. Most importantly, since becoming a Christian, he has been in continuous study of God's Word and Jesus Christ. Against that "plumb line," Manuel measures all else he learns. As he studies and gleans, he readily shares with his players not only the keys to succeeding in the game, but also key life lessons.

There is only one true source of wisdom. Proverbs tells us that *the fear of the Lord is the beginning of wisdom* and that *wisdom is supreme; therefore get wisdom* even though it may *cost all you have* (1:7;4:7). Knowledge is good, but wisdom is better. Many of us operate in knowledge, but how many of us operate in wisdom? God once told Solomon He would give him the one thing he wanted most. Solomon's request: wisdom. God gave Solomon not only wisdom but also the fruit that comes when one pursues wisdom. Pursue wisdom; seek after it even if there is seemingly great cost in doing so. You will find that God will give you His wisdom, and with it the fullness of life.

Blessed is the man who finds wisdom, the man who gains understanding, for she [wisdom] *is more profitable than silver and yields better returns than gold. She is more precious than rubies; nothing you desire can compare with her. She is a tree of life to those who embrace her; those who lay hold of her will be blessed.*

—Proverbs 3:13-15,18

"You can't let go."

Excellence:

Champions give everything they have to become the best they can be.

One of the greatest pure hitters of his era, Edgar Martinez is not normally spoken of when discussing the game's superstars. Perhaps it is because he has spent most of his career as a designated hitter. Perhaps it is because he has played his entire career in Seattle, tucked away in the upper northwestern corner of the United States, where nightly stats don't make it to the eastern markets before bedtime. Perhaps it is because throughout his career he has been overshadowed by other superstars—Ken Griffey Jr., Randy Johnson, and Alex Rodriguez. But inside the baseball circles, where it really counts, he is known.

The men who play the game day in and day out, as well as the men who coach the game, all know that Edgar Martinez is the finest right-handed hitter of the past decade. They also know that he is the game's hardest worker. The two-time American League batting champion has been a consistent .300 plus hitter throughout his career. But it hasn't come without an intense dedication to his craft. He is tireless in the batting cage and is consistently found out on the field early taking extra batting practice. Prior to games, it is common to see players from opposing teams come out to watch Edgar take batting practice.

Profile of Edgar Martinez

"Edgar is a very hard worker," said his former M's hitting coach Gene Clines. "He does a lot of work underneath in the batting cage that people don't see. He spends an enormous amount of time with the hitting tee. He made himself into [a] good hitter."

Martinez always seems to be busy. If he's not on the field, he's likely to be swinging in the cage. If he's not swinging a bat, he's probably riding a stationary bike. While other players are sleeping into the early afternoon after a night game, Martinez hops out of bed while it is still morning, puts on his swim trunks, and jumps into the pool for a series of aquatic arm and leg exercises. All the work pays off.

"Edgar is unbelievable," says former teammate Alex Rodriguez. "His work ethic is second to none. I've learned so much from him. He is the godfather. Everything I know, I know from him."

"I'm amazed at the way he works," says Mariners outfielder Mike Cameron. "It drives me every day. I'm still trying to get myself to a position where I'm molded to that point."

Because of his work ethic, among Latin players, Martinez is known as "El Papa"—the godfather of hitting. During the winter, dozens of young Latin hopefuls gather at Martinez's home early each morning to learn from him, to work out with him, or just watch him work out. To these kids it is like watching a master artist—a da Vinci of baseball. "He's a role model for me," says Kevin Robles, a prospect from Martinez's hometown of Dorado, Puerto Rico. "He would show me the value of sports, and what to do off the field—not be on the streets late, not drinking, working hard and working for what you want in life."

"He's like a father, a grandfather, El Papa," says former Yankees infielder Luis Sojo. "As a player, as a man, he's a role model for all of us."

"When you're young the season ends, and you can take two months off to relax," says Martinez. "Now I take one week. When you're older, [your] body starts to go. You have to do everything you can to fight that. You can't let go."

The Heart of a Champion will not settle for good when the best is still attainable:

Edgar Martinez has been one of baseball's great hitters into his forties. The reason, he continues to work at hitting. While some athletes rest in their past success, Edgar realizes he still has room to grow and improve. So he goes back to work—rare at this age for an individual who has reached the top to keep pushing to get better. Yet that is the attitude of a champion.

Do you know what is the single greatest enemy of becoming the best? It's not doubters, critics, or adversity. Rather, it is becoming good. Good is always the enemy of best. When we discover that we are proficient or good at something, we tend to stop there and realize our achievements. When we do this, we will never discover the best. Becoming satisfied with the good will always keep us from God's best for us. We must keep pushing onward, seeking the better and aiming for the best. God always has more for us—more to grow in, more to know, more to experience, more to accomplish, more to love. He has the best for you. Don't miss it by settling for "good."

Do your best to present yourself to God as one approved, a workman who does not need to be ashamed and who correctly handles the word of truth.

—2 Timothy 2:15

Profile of PEDRO MARTINEZ

"I know where I come from; a poor family from a poor country. My family taught me the value of staying humble. They were more interested in Pedro the person than Pedro the pitcher. That's why I don't like to talk about the money or the fame . . . . God is number one."

COMPASSION:

A champion gives to others.

A few hours before he leaves the Dominican Republic each February for spring training with the Boston Red Sox, the best pitcher in the American League stops briefly to visit the church he built in his hometown of Manoguayabo. For Pedro Martinez, it is always a poignant moment, reminding him where he has come from and refocusing him on what his life is all about.

The church, The Immaculate Conception, is a basic concrete structure with a steeple. It sits on a hill surrounded by dirt roads and cinder-block houses that make up Manoguayabo, a rural town of 5,000, where the main jobs are in the sugarcane fields.

Martinez, a three-time Cy Young Award winner and his league's most dominant pitcher during the late 1990s and early part of the twenty-first century, paid to have the church constructed.

"The church was a dream that I had since I was a kid," Martinez said. "It was something that I felt that I had to do for my hometown and my people."

Martinez was compelled to build the church, he says, as a demonstration of extended arms to the people of his community and out of a sense of gratitude toward God.

"Getting a chance to achieve so many things that I wasn't expecting in life, I've been blessed," he says. "To me that's probably the most important thing; showing people that and reaching out and helping other people. You're going to feel satisfaction for yourself and you're also giving other people a chance that they didn't expect to have. The church was my way to let the people know that God exists, and they should believe God helped me throughout my career."

The church opened in 1998 and held its first service just as Martinez was catching a plane to Florida to begin spring training with the Red Sox that year. He remembers the emotion he felt as he saw his dream completed.

"It was beautiful, the painting of the walls, the decorations," he recalls. "I didn't talk. I didn't touch anything. I felt realized. It was something I wanted to do long before I signed the contract.

"When I was growing up, the town didn't have its own church. The closest church was maybe three or four miles away. That's [a] little far to have to walk."

Thanks to the generosity of Martinez, the people of his hometown do not have the long walk to church anymore. Nor do they have trouble finding a baseball field. Martinez also built a public sports complex with a gym and several ball fields for local youngsters, hoping to bring them brighter days and demonstrating that for him life is about more than money and pitching honors.

"My last name is worth more than money," he said. "I never want to let my family down for whatever money you can offer. I never see a dollar bill throw a pitch. It is humans who pitch. I never think of the money.

"I know where I come from; a poor family from a poor country. My family taught me the value of staying humble. They were more interested in Pedro the person than Pedro the pitcher. That's why I don't like to talk about the money or the fame. I want to give to the other people the chance that I never got. I think I realize that money is just material, and everything passes by, including yourself. I try to do the best I can for the people to understand that God is number one."

The Heart of a Champion gives unselfishly to those in need:

Pedro Martinez's dream of building a church in his hometown was fulfilled because he never gave up on that dream. His desire was to give of his own resources to benefit others who did not have the means to build a church. In giving of himself, Martinez received a great blessing in return, enabling thousands to be exposed to the same source that has given his own life meaning. In giving once, he provided for many. Those who now have a better life because of him will remember Pedro Martinez for what he gave to them long after they have forgotten his pitching records.

Many people who are in the public eye talk about wanting to help others. Some make charitable contributions either to causes that are chic or take little effort to pursue. In the case of Martinez, he truly lived up to his words by giving what was needed and tackling the entire effort himself. How often do we talk about helping people in need, but when it comes down to it, the words are not backed up by action? How often do we tell people we will pray for their personal need, only to walk away and forget to take action? The Bible tells us that faith without action is dead. The world is tired of talk, tired of hearing about the message of Christ. However, they desperately want to see a demonstration of the reality of the life of Christ in us. Pedro has done that. How about you?

What good is it, my brothers, if a man claims to have faith but has no deeds? . . . Suppose a brother or sister is without clothes and daily food. If one of you says to him, "Go, I wish you well; keep warm and well fed," but does nothing about his physical needs, what good is it? In the same way, faith by itself, if it is not accompanied by action, is dead.

—James 2:14-17

Profile of PAUL MOLITOR

It came down to knowing there was no better way to finish my career than in front of family and friends."

PERSPECTIVE:

A champion values what is most important.

Paul Molitor always had a special place in his heart for the Minnesota Twins. When Molitor was a child, his father, Richard, used to take him to old Metropolitan Stadium in suburban Bloomington for his birthday and on the special "Knot Hole" days for kids at the ballpark. They sat together in the upper deck in left field, with Paul usually wearing his favorite Harmon Killebrew T-shirt.

Like many other fans, Molitor would lie awake at night, listening to Twins broadcasters Herb Cornell and Halsey Hall describe the feats of Killebrew and other Twins greats. He would play ball in his backyard, pretending he was outfielder Bob Allison. He used to write for autographs from the Twins and started a collection in his room: Mudcat Grant . . . Earl Battey . . . Tony Oliva . . . Don Mincher . . . Camilo Pascual.

"Growing up, I lived and died with the Twins," Molitor says. "Even when I got to the major leagues, I still followed them. I read the box scores and knew most of the players. I never forgot my connection to the Twins."

Living just five blocks away from Molitor at the time was the king of the local playground, Dave Winfield, who was four years older than Molitor. "His athleticism was legendary down there," says Molitor. "I never played on the same team with him, but when I was in eighth grade I worked out with his Legion team. What a thrill."

Attucks-Brooks American Legion Post 606 won back-to-back state titles in 1967-68 with Winfield as the star, then won again in 1974 with Molitor leading the way.

Those early years foreshadowed the greatness that emerged during Molitor's Hall of Fame career. He spent 21 seasons combined with the Milwaukee Brewers and Toronto Blue Jays, where he displayed great consistency and became one of baseball's greatest all-time hitters. In the 1993 World Series, at age thirty-seven, Molitor was named World Series MVP in leading the Blue Jays to victory.

Then in 1996, at age thirty-nine, Molitor was closing in on the 3,000-hit standard. Several teams were trying to sign him for the last few seasons of his career.

Still, the St. Paul native turned down pennant contenders in Baltimore and Cleveland, as well as former employers in Milwaukee and Toronto, and more money, to sign a two-year deal with his beloved Minnesota Twins.

"Having all my family here made it easier," Molitor said of the decision. "There were things you used to miss out on when everybody else was together. . . . It came down to knowing there was no better way to finish my career than in front of family and friends," he says. "Even if I went to the team with the best chance of winning, I would always regret not finishing up in Minnesota."

On September 16, 1996, he notched career hit 3,000, the first man ever to do so, by hitting a triple, and he finished with 3,319 hits, eighth all-time in baseball history. He played two more seasons before retiring after the 1998 season at age forty-two. He retired, as he had grown up, attached to the Minnesota Twins.

The Heart of a Champion places value on life at home:

Born and raised in rural Minnesota, Paul Molitor loved the simple life, baseball, and the Minnesota Twins. At the end of his great major league career, he determined that he would complete his career in the place he grew up. For Molitor, there was something comforting—something right—about going home. The money was not important; neither was the opportunity to be on a competitive team. What mattered most was the homecoming. Molitor longed to play for the team that he had loved as a kid and to play in front of the fans with whom he had once cheered. He simply wanted to go home.

There is something inside all of us that longs for home. Those who are Christ-followers are eager to see Him face-to-face. At some point, those who have wandered away want to find their way home. Where are you? When God spoke to Adam in the Garden after the first sin, He asked, "Adam, where are you?" Did God not know where Adam was? Of course God knew—but Adam did not. Adam did not understand where he was in relation to the God who had created him. Once he understood, he longed to return "home." The prodigal longed to return home as well, and upon doing so, he was met with a warm and loving reception. In some way, in some area of our lives, we are all prodigals. If you are away, no matter where you are, no matter what you've done, the Father longs for you to "come home" and be restored to your place as a child of the King.

"So he got up and went to his father. But while he was still a long way off, his father saw him and was filled with compassion for him; he ran to his son, threw his arms around him and kissed him. . . . 'Let's have a feast and celebrate. For this son of mine was dead and is alive again; he was lost and is found.'"

—Luke 15:20, 23-24

Profile of JOHNNY OATES

"I haven't always balanced baseball and life. Unfortunately, my family had to suffer for me to learn that baseball can be very, very important to us, but it can't be the only thing in our lives."

SACRIFICE:

A champion places family first.

During his four seasons of managing the Baltimore Orioles, Johnny Oates won 291 games and lost 270. His last three clubs went 237-189, the seventh best mark in the major leagues over that span. Nonetheless, following the 1994 season, Orioles owner Peter Angeles fired him.

The Texas Rangers were all too happy to bring Oates aboard to replace the departing Bobby Valentine. Oates was looking forward to the challenges of rejoining his friend, Texas General Manager Doug Melvin, to build the Rangers into a contender. Little did Oates know that he was about to be hit by a family crisis that had been looming on the horizon for years.

"I haven't always balanced baseball and life," says Oates. "Unfortunately, my family had to suffer for me to learn that baseball can be very, very important to us, but it can't be the only thing in our lives. We in professional sports get so spoiled sometimes with the red carpet treatment we get everywhere we go. We become immune to the needs of our wives, our families. . . . Our kids suffered a lot. My wife suffered a lot. I finally came to realize that I can still enjoy baseball, but it's not the only thing in my life."

On the afternoon of April 15, 1995, just weeks into his new job, Oates hopped into his car, tore out of Port Charlotte, the Rangers spring training home, not knowing if he would ever return. He jumped onto Interstate 75 and headed north out of Florida toward Savannah, Georgia. That was as far as his wife, Gloria, had made it from Colonial Heights, Virginia, on her way to Florida for a visit with her husband. The daily pressures of carrying the family alone had overwhelmed Gloria. She was hospitalized for what Oates has said was "emotional and physical exhaustion."

Jerry Narron, Oates' third-base coach, took charge of the team. Both Melvin and Tom Schieffer, the Rangers president, told Oates to stay with his wife as long as he was needed. Instead of getting in the car and returning to Florida, Oates drove his family home to Virginia. Gloria Oates checked into a Richmond hospital. Johnny told the Rangers he wouldn't be coming back for a while. Gloria went for counseling. Johnny went for counseling. They talked. They listened. Decades of silence were broken.

It ended up as a sixteen-day leave of absence, but at the time no one was sure if Oates would ever be seen again wearing a Texas uniform. He has since told friends that in the depth of Gloria's illness, he offered to resign as the Rangers manager. The season had begun without him. It would continue without him. He began planning life without baseball.

That willingness to walk away from his career, Oates has said, became a turning point in his wife's recovery. After Johnny told her of his decision to give it all up, Gloria's condition improved almost overnight. Soon Oates felt that his wife was well enough for him to return to work. "That had to be really tough on him," says Melvin. "Not many people know what he went through and how tough it was."

For ten days, Gloria Oates watched her husband. Finally she told him he should return to his team. "Go back," Oates says his wife told him. "Baseball is not your mistress anymore."

Oates returned to baseball, but only after the couple solidified a commitment to talk on a daily basis, regardless of where they might be. The phone calls ranged from one hour to three. "We had an agreement that we would call each other at 4:30 in the morning if we had to," Oates remembered.

On the field, Oates experienced his finest seasons, leading the Rangers to three division titles and averaging 85 wins per season. More than that, he was enjoying the fruits of a healthy balance of family and baseball. For Oates, it couldn't have come at a better time.

In spring of 2001 the conversations became much more regular, when Oates stepped down as the headman of the Rangers. Later that year Johnny would learn he was battling a vigorous brain tumor. The family had come to cherish the changes that had taken place since that day in 1995 and were thankful for the time that had been provided.

The Heart of a Champion makes family the number-one earthly priority:

Johnny Oates had a great career, a great salary, a great office, and great benefits. But he had a miserable family. When Oates learned of the seriousness of the situation, he made a move to find a solution. His move was unprecedented. He had not even started the season yet with his new team, but he left it all behind to go after his wife and salvage his family. His career had nearly cost him his family, so he determined to save his family at *any* cost. Oates recognized that if he lost his family he would have nothing that mattered.

Today, in our culture, the sense of priority demonstrated by Oates seems to be reversed. Men and women are willing to sacrifice their families at the altars of success and in the pursuit of personal fulfillment. Divorce rates have skyrocketed, and many have tried marriage multiple times, but often compatibility must take second place to the job. So many today have virtual mistresses—computers, office desks, telephones, PDAs, fax machines, pagers, cell phones. At every turn they vie for our attention all in the name of climbing the ladder of success. Left behind are the people who are most important—our spouses and children. They suffer from feeling disconnected and lonely and wait to be rescued from a slow emotional death. Could you do what Johnny Oates did—drop *everything* and run to save your family? Honestly, would you do it if you found yourself faced with the same situation? Now, will you, when you are? In some way, it will happen, and you will be faced with a choice of what you value most. When that day comes, what will you do?

Do not conform any longer to the pattern of this world, but be transformed by the renewing of your mind. Then you will be able to test and approve what God's will is—his good, pleasing and perfect will.

—Romans 12:2

"The Lord is making me mature and complete. He's molding me into the image of Christ, and that's encouraging. . . . He can work anything for our good.

COURAGE:

A champion overcomes.

F our years before he would become the American League batting champion, John Olerud faced the prospect of his prime being cut cruelly short.

In the winter before his junior season at Washington State University, the All-American pitcher/first baseman began to suffer brief, fifteen-second episodes of severe pain in his head. Then, while jogging to get ready for the team's timed-mile run, he blacked out. John's father, John Olerud Sr., was a doctor at University of Washington Medical Center. He sent his son in for a full battery of tests, which at first ruled out tumors, viruses, and infection. X rays showed nothing unusual. But a colleague of Dr. Olerud's at UWMC suggested that John be x-rayed at other angles. John, ready to start the baseball season in Pullman, reluctantly flew to Seattle for further observation.

"The guy brings out the X ray, and I go, 'There it is'," recalls John. "You didn't have to be a brain surgeon to pick it out."

The new X rays revealed a brain aneurysm—a blood-filled sac that forms on a swollen blood vessel. Had the aneurysm not been detected, there was a 50 percent chance it would have ruptured and killed John instantly.

On February 27, 1989, John Sr. and his wife, Lynda, drove to Harborview Medical Center in Seattle with their son, who prepared for brain surgery by flipping through the sports pages. Seven weeks after the operation, major league star-to-be John Olerud was back in the Cougar lineup. Though twenty pounds lighter and wobbly-legged, he wound up his junior season with a 3-2 pitching record and a .359 batting average. He finished the regular season with a flourish against Gonzaga, tossing a five-hitter and mashing two homers in a doubleheader. He was drafted by the Toronto Blue Jays two weeks later. Six days after signing with Toronto, Olerud was in the big leagues—the sixteenth player since the amateur draft began in 1965 to go directly from amateur ball to the major leagues.

"I was fortunate in that I never played an inning in the minor leagues," John says. "My major league debut came on September 3, 1989—the same year I had brain surgery."

His debut was like a scene from *The Natural.* "It was practically a religious experience watching him in Toronto that first day of batting practice," recalls the senior Olerud. "The Skydome opened up right when he started hitting with the light streaming down."

The light has continuously been on Olerud since that very first day. One of the game's top hitting and fielding first basemen, he has been honored with Gold Glove Awards and won the batting title in 1993, hitting .363. He was also a key member of the Blue Jays World Series champs in 1992 and 1993. He helped the New York Mets make it to the play-offs, before going back home to play for the Seattle Mariners in 2000.

His trademark, along with his sweet swing, is the helmet Olerud wears at all times—even in the field. It is part protection for the area that was once the source of Olerud's greatest challenge and part reminder of what he has overcome.

"I really feel that God spared me in that incident, because I can't tell you how many people I've met that know somebody that died from something like that," says Olerud. "I've met lots of kids in the hospitals who've had to learn to walk again and talk again and do a lot of rehab and that sort of thing. So I feel like the Lord definitely spared me.

"The Lord is making me mature and complete. He's molding me into the image of Christ, and that's encouraging. Romans 8:28 says that He can work all things for good to those who love the Lord. He can work anything for our good. Sometimes when we just can't figure out what the purpose of the trial is or how any good could come of it, that's definitely reassuring."

The Heart of a Champion is grateful for growth through adversity:

John Olerud lived through a harrowing experience, nearly dying on the very field he had hoped would provide the setting for his future. Yet, in trauma, Olerud came through his experience with nothing but feelings of gratitude for being given a chance for a future. Rather than becoming bitter about the suffering he experienced, he became more determined to see his life used to the fullest for his remaining days, regardless of their length. The experience served to strengthen Olerud's resolve and build his courage. He knew his trial had a purpose of making him a more mature and finer person. As such, Olerud has become a living example of God's grace.

Every person experiences trials of some sort during their life-time. Yet it is not the trials that define a person, but rather their response to those trials. Typically, we are given to one of two responses—either thankfulness for all that we have been given or bitterness at what has befallen us. While God is not the author of trials, we often hold Him responsible and even express our ire with a seemingly cavalier approach to our circumstances.

Yet the truth is God cares so deeply for you, that when you hurt, He hurts as well. His heart desires that none would suffer, but in His grace, He turns suffering and trials into a refining fire that molds and shapes your character quite unlike any other experience. He uses each ember to make you mature and complete, lacking in nothing. In that way, trials become well worth the outcome.

Consider it pure joy, my brothers, whenever you face trials of many kinds, because you know that the testing of your faith develops perseverance. Perseverance must finish its work so that you may be mature and complete, not lacking anything.

—James 1:2-4

Profile of CURTIS PRIDE

The crowd at Olympic Stadium gave him a five-minute standing ovation. "It brought tears to my eyes," Pride says. "It still does. . . . It's something I'll never forget."

PERSEVERANCE:

Champions see themselves through the eyes of God.

I n 1994, then Montreal Expos outfielder Curtis Pride was named one of the ten "Outstanding Young Americans" of the year by the United States Junior Chamber of Commerce. Pride, who has bounced back and forth between baseball's major and minor leagues for fifteen years, is legally deaf. In 1993 he became the first deaf person to play in the majors in more than fifty years.

His seven major league season totals entering 2003 are respectable for any player, amazing for one who can't hear. In 349 games, he has hit .256 with 18 home runs, 76 RBIs, and 28 stolen bases. His best season came for the Detroit Tigers in 1996, when he appeared in 95 games, hitting .300, with 10 home runs and 31 RBIs.

Hearing loss is categorized as mild, moderate, severe, or profound. Pride's is considered profound. He was a victim of the nationwide rubella outbreak in 1968. His mother, Sallie, contracted German measles during her pregnancy. The family also has two daughters who can hear.

"It could have been worse," Pride said. "I could have been blind or retarded or born with some deformity."

Pride wears a hearing aid in his left ear, but he communicates by reading lips and then forming words he has never heard. He must be directly faced when addressed, but conversation comes much more freely than most expect. Pride does not use sign language.

"He can hear sound when it's amplified, but it just sounds like noise," explained his father, John Pride. "He can't actually distinguish what the sound is without the lip cues."

In seventh grade Pride insisted on attending a neighborhood school in Silver Spring, Maryland, rather than one with special programs for the hearing impaired. He ended up graduating from John F. Kennedy High with a 3.6 grade point average and starred in three sports. As a striker on the JFK soccer team, he earned Parade All America honors. As a point guard on the basketball team, he was offered a full scholarship to William & Mary. As an outfielder on the baseball team, he was selected by the New York Mets in the tenth round of the 1986 amateur draft.

Pride accepted the scholarship to William & Mary where he started as point guard and graduated with a degree in finance. Each summer between 1986 and 1990, he also played in the Met farm system, before turning his attention full time to baseball.

He is also giving back to provide the kind of help and inspiration he himself experienced. Pride is a spokesperson for the Better Hearing Institute and works during the off-season as a special education instructional assistant. He frequently speaks at schools and organizations around the country.

Pride's shining moment came in his major league debut in Montreal in 1993. In his second at bat, Pride's two-run double helped the Expos rally to an 8-7 victory against Philadelphia. The crowd at Olympic Stadium gave him a five-minute standing ovation.

"It brought tears to my eyes," Pride says. "It still does. I have it on videotape. It's something I'll never forget."

The Heart of a Champion views everyone else as equals:

One of the things that is so refreshing about Curtis Pride is the fact that he does not view himself as being any different from anyone else. Although Pride has a physical disability, it is clear that he does not desire sympathy or special treatment because of his condition. Rather, Pride has worked hard so that others view him as an equal. He does not see himself as disadvantaged but instead feels fortunate that his situation is not worse. To him, the "playing field" is level, and as such he has not looked for concessions. Rather than espousing a "woe is me" attitude, Pride has taken the approach that if he gives it his all, nothing should hold him back.

How do you view yourself? Do you see yourself as God sees you or as the world views you? Everyone has some sort of struggle. No matter what you face, you must never lose sight of the fact that God loves you and has a purpose and a destiny for your life that is totally unique. Rather than identifying the ways that you are "different" from others around you, keep pressing on and seeking after the unique plan God has for you. The Bible tells us that each of us is His "workmanship," or literally, His *masterpiece.* No challenge, adversity, failure, or disability can ultimately deter you from God's plan, nor separate you from His love.

We are God's workmanship, created
in Christ Jesus to do good works, which
God prepared in advance for us to do.

—Ephesians 2:10

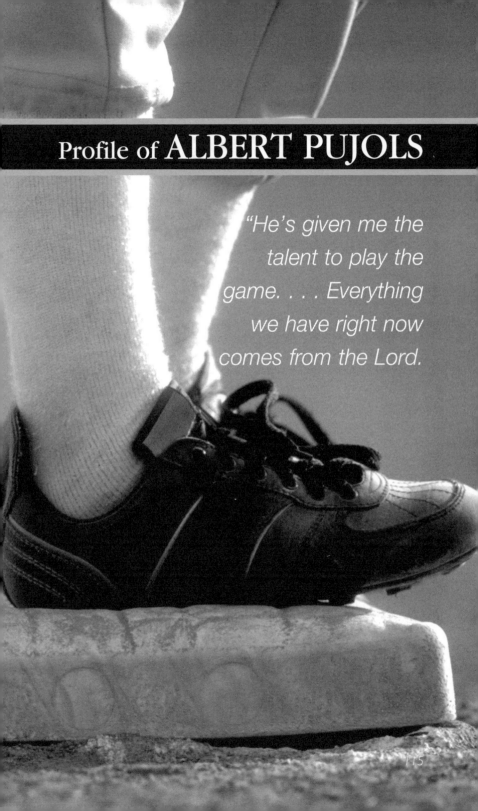

Profile of ALBERT PUJOLS

"He's given me the talent to play the game. . . . Everything we have right now comes from the Lord."

PRIORITIES:

Champions do not let success change them.

At the start of the 2000 season, Albert Pujols was twenty years old, fresh out of junior college, toiling away at Class A Peoria in his first year in professional baseball. By the end of 2001, he was hitting .329, with 37 home runs, 130 RBIs, and 112 runs scored for the St. Louis Cardinals, in what was one of the most remarkable rookie seasons in baseball history. He was honored as the National League Rookie of the Year and finished fourth in the league's MVP voting. His encore in 2002 was equally superb as he hit .314 with 34 homers, 127 RBIs, and 118 runs scored.

Prior to 2001 Pujols was largely unheard of. Much of the outfielder's opportunity for success came with a change in his address.

Things had changed dramatically for Pujols when he turned sixteen. At an age when most American youth are eagerly eyeing a driver's license, Pujols was looking at a new life. Born and raised in Santo Domingo, Dominican Republic, Pujols was the youngest of twelve children in a family, typical in the impoverished baseball-loving country. But Pujols' father decided to move to the United States and bring his son with him. They settled in the Kansas City area, and Pujols enrolled at Fort Osage High School, where he became a two-time all-state performer for Fort Osage and then played at Maple Woods Community College in Kansas City. He was selected by the Cardinals in the thirteenth round of the 1999 draft.

Profile of Albert Pujols

After his one season in the minor leagues in 2000, Pujols was invited to spring training in 2001, where the Cardinals decided to give him exposure to a big league camp. He played so well in the spring, however, that the team could not break camp without him on the major league squad. So, at twenty-one, with just one season of minor league baseball under his belt, Pujols began his major league career, comparing notes with the likes of Mark McGwire.

His first two seasons were historic, as he became the first player in major league baseball history to hit over .300 and collect 30 or more home runs, 100 or more RBIs, and 100 or more runs in his first two seasons. His 2001 totals set national league rookie records for RBIs and total bases, with his home run total falling just one short of the national league rookie record. A star was born.

There was little chance that any of this could have happened had Pujols not accompanied his father to the U.S. There was also little chance that Pujols would have been ready to handle his success without his wife, Deidre, whom he met in 1998 and married on New Year's Day 2000. At the start of their relationship, Deidre told Albert of her faith in Christ as the foundation for her life. Though he had gone to church occasionally while growing up, Pujols made a decision to become a Christian. The change gave him a profound sense of thankfulness and helped him keep perspective in the midst of success.

"He's given me the talent to play the game," Pujols says. "If it wasn't for Him, I don't think I would have been here today. Everything we have right now comes from the Lord. All the credit for the success I've had with the Cardinals is going to Him, every single at-bat."

That realization has inspired a desire to give back. "The Dominican Republic is a poor country," Pujols says, ever aware of his beginnings. "I asked God that if I ever got to play here, when I got the money, I wanted to help the country out. That's one of the main things; I want to help the country out."

The Heart of a Champion understands the source of all that is good:

Albert Pujols has had startling success. To play one year in the minor leagues and then to dominate major league pitching makes it seem as though what he has done is easy. But Pujols has a sense of calm about him. He is not caught up in his accomplishments because he realizes he is not responsible for his prowess. Pujols understands that all he has comes from God. Knowing this frees Pujols to just go out and play without pressure. It's not that he doesn't care—he cares very much, which is why he prepares and studies—but he doesn't carry the pressure to succeed. Pujols realizes that God will derive the most out of his abilities.

How difficult it is for us to demonstrate real faith when things are going well. But in trials, boy do we need God to intervene! When things go well, it is easy for us to take credit and switch over to autopilot. We think we are doing a pretty good job, and we become less vigilant about areas of weakness. Typically, these are the very times when we are most susceptible to temptation. When things are going well, we need to continue to thank God, recognizing that every good thing comes from Him alone. Then we must remain alert to the attack of pride and self-sufficiency—enemies waiting to take us out.

He said to me, "My grace is sufficient for you,
for my power is made perfect in weakness."
Therefore I will boast all the more gladly about
my weaknesses, so that Christ's power may rest
on me. . . . For when I am weak, then I am strong.

—2 Corinthians 12:9-10

Profile of PEE WEE REESE

*"If he's man enough
to take my job,
I'm not gonna like it,
but, black or white,
he deserves it."*

COMPASSION:

A champion stands for what is right.

I t was a simple gesture, really. Nothing was even spoken in the process. Yet the effect of the act went far beyond what a thousand words could have conveyed.

It happened on May 14, 1947, at a typical Wednesday afternoon baseball game at Cincinnati's Crosley Field, where the hometown Reds were getting ready to take on the hated Brooklyn Dodgers. Only on this afternoon, as with so many others in the early season, the Dodgers had one more reason than usual to be hated. For wearing the #42 Brooklyn uniform and playing the infield that day was a black man named Jackie Robinson.

But it was right there on the grounds of Crosley that day, the 30,000 or so businessmen and kids who sneaked away from their offices and schools were witness to one of the most profound moments in baseball's long and storied lore.

Not all fans around the country were aware of the Dodgers decision to become the first team in history to place a black man on their roster. But as the fans at Crosley that day noticed Robinson on the field warming up among other players, a wave of racial strife and hatred began to emerge. Slowly, much of the crowd that had begun to fill the stadium began chanting the "N word" and hurling one derisive slur after another in the direction of the silent Robinson. Over and over the words echoed. Some fans stood and leaned over the railings of the stands, shaking their fists and shouting, "Get back to your own league, you black . . ." Scenes like this had been commonplace ever since Branch Rickey chose Robinson to break baseball's color barrier. But none had been this volatile, this hostile, this close to exploding into an even uglier scene. Soon, Reds players from various spots on the field and in the dugout joined in the barrage of abusive epithets. That's when it happened, a moment that would spark an indelible change in the sport.

Brooklyn's shortstop, then 29-year-old all-star, Pee Wee Reese, slowly walked from his position at shortstop across the diamond toward Robinson. When he arrived at first base, he dropped his glove and slowly, and very deliberately, put his arm around Robinson. Before the throng of angry fans, the white southerner Reese hugged the black Robinson. The two men chuckled a bit, and then Reese looked up at the bleachers. The stadium grew quiet. The moment is cited as a turning point in Robinson's transition.

Recalls longtime Dodgers broadcaster Vin Sculley, "That was a message sent to one and all that a boy from the South puts his arms around a black man and says, 'Hey, we're equal, we're teammates, and we're in this thing together.' And that was typical of Pee Wee."

"I've got a big picture of it, both of us laughing, hanging in my den," Reese said of the moment shortly before his death in 2000.

"Think of the guts that took," former Dodgers teammate Carl Erskine says in remembering that day. "Pee Wee had to go home [to segregated Louisville] and answer to his friends. I told Jackie later that [Reese's gesture] helped my race more than his."

In his 1972 best-selling book *The Boys of Summer*, author Roger Kahn hailed Reese as a "catalyst of baseball integration" for his friendship with Robinson. He writes of how Reese recalled that upon hearing that the Dodgers organization had hired a black man, he thought, *If he's man enough to take my job, I'm not gonna like it, but, black or white, he deserves it.*

Reese told Kahn that he was determined to do his part to help see Robinson's situation change. "There were times when I went over to talk to him on the field, thinking that people would see this and figure we were friends and this would help Jack."

Later, upon hearing of Reese's death, Kahn wrote of the man's character as reflected in that defining moment: "Reese detested bigotry, hatred against blacks or Jews or Latinos, whatever. I never knew anyone whose life was a more towering example of decency."

Pee Wee Reese was an eight-time all-star, the backbone of great Dodgers teams in the 1940s and 1950s. He sparked the Dodgers to seven national league pennants and led Brooklyn to its only World Series championship in 1955. In 1984 he was inducted into baseball's Hall of Fame. Only 5-feet-9-inches tall and 160 pounds, he never stood taller nor had a greater impact on the game of baseball than on that day in May of 1947.

The Heart of a Champion sends powerful messages:

Harold Pee Wee Reese was a champion. When he was eulogized at his funeral, it was said that baseball had lost a courageous person. Can you imagine what it must have been like to be in the stadium that day? What a turning point that moment must have provided, not just for Jackie Robinson but for so many people watching. White people.

Comfortable and complacent white people. Racists. White people who let others speak up while they found ways to conveniently keep silent. They just stood there together, a black ballplayer and a white ballplayer, and faced that thundering wall of hatred. Were there feelings of injustice? Certainly. Anger? To be sure. Reese's response was to take the most important steps of his professional career, from shortstop to first base. His actions defied the forces of prejudice and hate.

Abraham Lincoln, himself a fan of the game of baseball, once said, "With malice toward none; with charity for all; with firmness in the right, as God gives us to see the right. . . ." How do you see the right? The author Kahn explains how "Reese detested bigotry." How much did he detest it? Enough to take action and do something about it.

What about you? How much do you hate prejudice, injustice, or any other sin? Do you still laugh at the jokes? Or are you filled with enough righteous indignation to do something about it, as Reese did? We are told to walk the fine line of hating sin and loving the sinner. What does it mean to hate sin? There are indeed sins of commission and sins of omission. Our lack of response to sin often speaks volumes about our hearts.

In contrast, when we do act—when we fight back against sin itself and take a stand—most often that action speaks louder than any words we could muster. Be a champion. Take a stand.

Be on your guard; stand firm in the faith;
be men of courage; be strong. Do everything in love.

—1 Corinthians 16:13-14

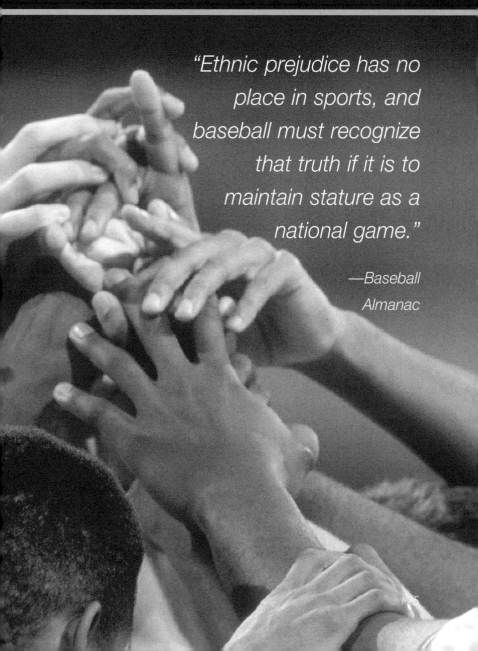

"Ethnic prejudice has no place in sports, and baseball must recognize that truth if it is to maintain stature as a national game."

—*Baseball Almanac*

LEADERSHIP:

Champions are willing to turn their backs to the crowd.

I n the world of baseball, Branch Rickey was a known genius, regardless of his role in the integration of the game with Jackie Robinson. An innovator, Rickey introduced baseball to the farm system, pitching machines, spring training complexes, and batting helmets. Clearly he was a man ahead of his time.

Rickey converted Stan Musial from a Class D pitcher to a Hall of Fame outfielder. He was the driving force behind expanding major league baseball to the western United States. He cofounded the Fellowship of Christian Athletes. He could have gone into the ministry, authored books, or "If he'd gone into politics," said Howard Green, general manager of the Dodgers farm club during Rickey's lifetime, "he could have been president."

In the midst of all the innovation and activity, Rickey desired to integrate baseball and, beyond that, American society. The idea first came to him as a coach at his alma mater, Ohio Wesleyan College. While the team was traveling to play other college teams, a black player named Charles Thomas was denied a hotel room in South Bend, Indiana. Only when Rickey intervened was he allowed a cot in Rickey's room. As Rickey told it, he later overheard Thomas crying and saw him pulling at his hands, as if he were wishing he could wipe off his pigmentation.

Rickey was motivated to make a difference and wanted to be on the cutting edge in this action, not just a follower. He had been looking for the right person to break the barrier for about three years. He asked prospective Dodgers players, "Would you ever have any objection to playing with a Negro?"

Some players did.

Rickey could have signed a lot of qualified players from the Negro Leagues, most with better baseball stature. But as Rickey said in a 1945 letter to Dr. Dan Dodson, who headed New York's Committee on Unity—an organization interested in promoting the integration of major league baseball—he had someone in mind who might not be the best player but fit best with Rickey's personality profile.

Rickey knew that the right man for the role in history was Jackie Robinson. So he signed him to a contract and told Robinson of his intentions. Then he prepared Jackie for what lay ahead.

After Robinson was promoted to the Dodgers, he did encounter opposition. But his skills and character eventually won over most. He was the perfect choice to break the color line. Robinson himself knew the importance of Rickey's actions, writing to him before he died, "It has been the finest experience I have had being associated with you; and I want to thank you very much for all you have meant, not only to me and my family but to the entire country and particularly the members of our race. I am glad for your sake that I had a small part to do with the success of your efforts, and I must admit, it was your constant guidance that enabled me to do so."

Though "the man who could have been president" never wound up in the White House, his legacy as one man who made the integration of baseball and the nation his priority ranks him every bit as influential as those who have occupied the oval office.

The Heart of a Champion knows that sometimes leadership means going it alone:

Think about Branch Rickey's situation. He knew that he needed to do something about the racism in baseball. He also knew that he had the respect of his peers and enough influence over them to take action. He also surmised that such a move could make him one of the most hated owners in sports and the most unpopular public figure in the nation.

Further, he knew that he would take action alone. When Rickey stood up to the system, he did so simply because it was the right thing to do, even though no other sports leader stood with him. Even alone, Rickey was a vehicle for radical change in our nation. This is the power of one choice, one action, one person standing firm under convictions from God. It is the power of one.

What do you see that makes you think, "Somebody needs to do something about this"? Is it a situation of inequity? A person being treated unfairly? A situation at your job or school that needs to be addressed? Whatever it is that stirs your passion, what are you going to do about it? "Me?" you say. Yes, you.

If God has stirred that passion in you, chances are that He wants you to do something about it. Is it to pray or to take some type of action? Only God knows, but He longs to show you so that you will take a step toward change. "What can I do?" you ask. A lot. Branch Rickey didn't know how far-reaching the effects of his actions would be; he merely did the one thing that he knew was right. That is the power of one person, making one choice, and taking one step toward change. Make a choice, take a step, and see things change. You have the power of one.

> *Jesus looked at them and said,*
> *"With man this is impossible, but not*
> *with God; all things are possible with God."*
>
> —Mark 10:27

Profile of MARIANO RIVERA

"The world give you fame, gives you a power, but the Lord gives you peace, and love. It's a love that nobody else can give you."

HUMILITY:

Champions never forget their beginnings.

He is perhaps the finest "closer" in all of major league baseball. His job is to enter games with runners on base and the game on the line. He is paid to protect the lead and save the game. To fail to do so, even for one in every four chances, means failure.

Yet in the midst of such intense pressure, Mariano Rivera never looks like a man in the pressure cooker. In fact, he always seems so cool that in staring down, say, Alex Rodriguez, or with the bases loaded, it seems like he is merely playing catch with his son.

That's because for this record-setting relief pitcher, closing out the World Series, as he did for the New York Yankees in 1998, 1999, and 2000, is nothing like the pressure he experienced as a youngster growing up in Panama. This man gained such perspective and strength as a boy, spending hours each day on a fishing boat captained by his father. Day after day they searched for sardines that would be sold at the marketplace to make fish flour.

"Sometimes we'd be out there a whole day and a whole night. Sometimes we don't catch nothing," says Rivera. "It was tough, but we survived."

Survival came because of the efforts of his father, Mariano Sr., who would not quit until he had provided for Mariano, his sister, and two brothers. It was a work ethic his son quickly emulated.

"If it wasn't for him," Rivera says of his father, "I don't think I would have this character. His character is strong, and he taught me that way."

Driven by his father's example, Rivera has become the most dominant relief pitcher in postseason history. But this only goes to show how far Rivera has come from his childhood years of poverty in the small Panamanian fishing town of Puerto Caimito.

There, when Rivera needed a baseball glove, he made one—from cardboard. He remembers fondly how much he learned from the days he used that makeshift glove, and the days when the fishing nets came up with far too light a load.

"That was the best time ever, the best childhood," he says. "I didn't miss anything. It was fun for me, the greatest thing that ever happened."

Now the slender 6-foot-2-inch, 170-pound right-hander, with the smooth delivery and exceptional fastball, is a hero back home, much as his father has been to him.

"When we [the Yankees] play, the city just shuts [down] completely. They're just watching the game," he says. "It's kind of neat."

The Heart of a Champion understands the significance of "small" things:

Mariano Rivera went from living in a poor fishing village to becoming the greatest relief pitcher in World Series history. Rather than regret his disadvantaged childhood, he remembers fondly the quality time spent with his family and the lessons of character he learned in those sparse beginnings. He believes it was that early life that prepared him to attain success in baseball without losing perspective. He also feels that his father's work ethic prepared him to pay the price to prepare for success.

We are exhorted not to despise the day of humble, or small, beginnings. Why? When you look back at where you started in life

Life Lessons from Baseball

in light of where you are today, how do you view those first days? Do you feel cheated? Or blessed? The humble beginnings had purpose. They were used by God to build some things in you that have helped bring you to this day. Nothing God does is insignificant or small. His hand has been molding, shaping, and refining your character so that you can reach the destiny He has for you with a humble and grateful heart. And so that you will fully recognize that all the credit in the process belongs to Him.

"Who despises the day of small things?"

—Zechariah 4:10

LEADERSHIP:

A champion mentors others.

Mariano Rivera is considered baseball's top relief pitcher. Through the 2002 season, he had helped the New York Yankees achieve four World Series titles and garnered a Series MVP trophy for his performance in 1999. He has already become the most prolific relief pitcher in the postseason in baseball history, with the major league record for most saves in the play-offs and World Series.

The native Panamanian was signed to a contract by the Yankees in 1990. Eleven years later he became the highest-paid relief pitcher in baseball history, signing a four-year contract worth $39.99 million. He throws a 95-mph cut fastball that moves what seems to be a foot across the strike zone. His slow, fluid windup seems to lull hitters into a relaxed state, and then suddenly his ball just jumps on top of the hitter. His cutter is tough for a batter to pick up, and many times if the hitter does make contact, the result is a shattered bat and a slow dribbler in the infield or a weak pop-up. By the end of the 2002 season, he had already recorded 243 career regular season saves and had become a main reason for the Yankees dominance since the mid-1990s.

Rivera is unshakeable on the mound. His expression almost never changes, and he exhibits a calmness that is noticed by his peers. Yankees shortstop Derek Jeter once said of his teammate, "Sometimes you can't tell if he's given up six hits in a row or just struck out six guys. There's no emotion from that guy out there. He just comes in, closes the door, and walks in the dugout."

Life Lessons from Baseball

But in Rivera's first experience in New York as a twenty-five-year-old rookie in 1995, he was anything but calm. He was the setup man for then closer John Wetteland and was a bit overwhelmed by life in the big leagues and life in the Big Apple. Rivera is quick to point out the influence his predecessor had on his life. Rivera watched as Wetteland became the game's premier closer with New York in the mid-1990s. He observed how Wetteland handled the attention and pressure of the media and how he dealt with heartbreaking failures and great successes, including the 1996 World Series MVP. Rivera watched Wetteland's demeanor and studied his character. He liked what he saw.

"John was like a teacher for me," Rivera says. "He was the first guy that I met who was a Christian. We talked a lot about the Bible, and about the game. I was a rookie [in 1995] and then in my second year in the big leagues, here I am, talking with the best closer. He came to be more of my friend, my family. That's why I say that year is special. That year just kind of opened up the way for me to go through."

Wetteland's example gave Rivera a model for how to approach his profession and his life.

"The world gives you fame, gives you a power; but the Lord gives you peace, and love," says Rivera. "It's a love that nobody else can give you. Not even the world can give you that."

That peace was never more evident than at the conclusion of the 2001 World Series. Rivera was on the mound as the Arizona Diamondbacks rallied in the bottom of the ninth inning to win game 7 and take the championship. It was the first time Rivera had either failed to save, or lost, a series game. Yet, much like his predecessor, he was mostly unfazed.

"Those are the major things as a pitcher you have to confront is blowing saves. And when I do that I have to forget everything. I even have to forget when I do [well], because it has passed already. I have to look forward and move on. And when I do that, everything else takes care of itself."

"God has helped me a lot to carry on in my life. Yes, this is what I love, but this will pass. This will pass and everything will be fine," he said of that moment. "You know, you win, you lose. When I lost the World Series, that was tough for me, but He gave me the peace. He gave me the strength to move on. And nobody will give me that. No man will give me that strength; will give me that peace, that love. He gave me that. That's why I move on."

The Heart of a Champion leads the way for others by demonstrating character:

Mariano Rivera's transformation from timid a rookie to a feared, composed, dominant closer is much less the result of an explosive cut fastball and best attributed to the example of John Wetteland. It was Wetteland who showed Rivera how to handle all the intricacies that come with being in the high-pressure role of a closer. From Wetteland, Rivera learned how to prepare physically and mentally. Rivera watched and studied, then put into practice all that he had learned. It is clear to Rivera that without his mentor, the success he has had would not have been possible.

God's plan for the teaching and training of mankind is quite clear. Jesus, our model, mentored those He brought around Him. The men and women observed Him carefully as they spent time with Him. They watched Him handle challenges, people, problems, and relationships. The character they saw in Him they integrated into their own lives. This is mentoring and, in fact, true discipleship. It is said that life lessons are "caught" rather than "taught." It is true that when we spend time with others, and they observe our choices and responses, they learn in a much greater way than through what we say. Who are you mentoring? Who is observing you and "catching" life lessons from you? What kind of a mentor are you for them? Are you helping them to become a champion?

Life Lessons from Baseball

Similarly, encourage the young men to be self-controlled.
In everything set them an example by doing what is good.
In your teaching show integrity, seriousness and
soundness of speech that cannot be condemned,
so that those who oppose you may be ashamed
because they have nothing bad to say about us.

—- Titus 2:6-8

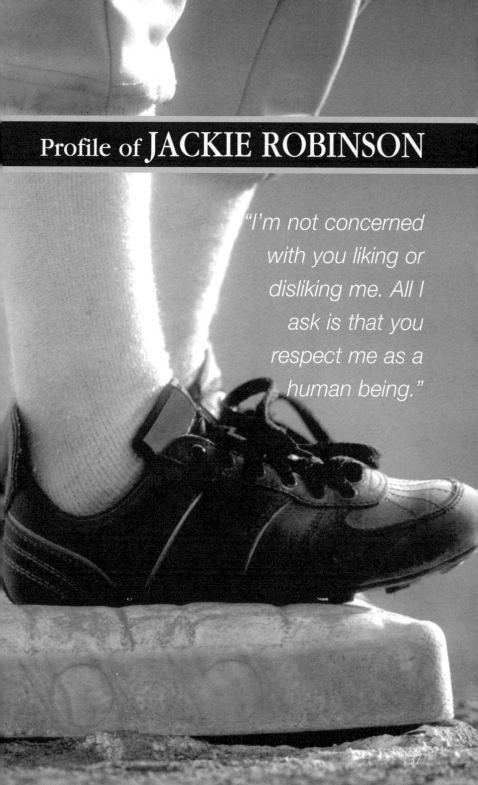

Profile of JACKIE ROBINSON

"I'm not concerned with you liking or disliking me. All I ask is that you respect me as a human being."

COURAGE:

A champion does what is right, no matter the cost.

On April 15, 1947, Jackie Robinson crossed the white chalk line that outlined the baseball diamond, and with it, the line of color separation that kept America's game in the bondage of bigotry. But Robinson didn't just break baseball's color barrier by becoming the first black major leaguer of the century. He also set into motion sweeping social changes. For the first time, America had a black hero at the very center of its consciousness. More than talent, it was Robinson's resolve and extraordinary self-control that made it possible.

Brooklyn Dodgers president, Branch Rickey, signed Robinson intending him to be the torchbearer for baseball integration. Rickey prepared his young player for the barrage he would have to endure in 1947, knowing that the first black player would have to survive all manner of provocation—emotional and physical. In Robinson, he saw a man with the fortitude to withstand the harshest opposition.

Robinson endured the most vicious treatment any athlete has ever faced. He was the target of racial epithets and flying cleats, of hate letters and death threats, of pitchers throwing at his head and legs, and catchers spitting on his shoes. In the midst of this chaos, there was a circus-like quality to Dodgers games, with Robinson on display. Large crowds, including many African-Americans, cheered his pop-ups and groundouts. The daily papers singled him out by use of racial monikers rather than by name. "More eyes were on

Jackie than on any rookie who ever played" recalls Rex Barney, a Brooklyn reliever that year.

The pressure increased. Police investigated letters that threatened Robinson's life. "He turned them over to me," announced Rickey. "Two of the notes were so vicious that I felt they should be investigated." The pressure also involved Robinson's lodging. In Philly the players usually stayed at the Benjamin Franklin Hotel; but when they arrived there, the hotel manager turned them away, telling the team's traveling secretary, Harold Parrott, "Don't bring your team back here while you have any Nigras with you!" The Dodgers stayed at the Warrick. Parrott later wrote that Robinson looked pained over the incident, "knowing we were pariahs because of him."

In the midst of such turmoil, Robinson soldiered on. "I'm just going along playing the best ball I know and doing my best to make good," he said. "Boy, it's rugged."

Robinson eventually won over most observers. He was named National League Rookie of the Year in 1947, and went on to be voted the league's MVP two years later. During his ten seasons, the Dodgers won six pennants, and a world championship. He was the team's catalyst, a second baseman who found numerous ways to beat the opponent. He was daring and exuded a competitive fire. He won a batting title, drove in 100 runs in a season, stole home 19 times, and hardly ever struck out.

Robinson's middle infield partner, shortstop Harold "Pee Wee" Reese, remembering his friend's display of courage, said, "I don't know any other ballplayer who could have done what he did—to be able to hit with everybody yelling at him. He had to block all that out. To do what he did has got to be the most tremendous thing I've ever seen in all of sports."

"I'm not concerned with you liking or disliking me," Robinson said. "All I ask is that you respect me as a human being." Respect came from the entire nation, as did admiration. Robinson not only carried the future of the game on his back but also the future of an entire people. The sense of burden was not lost on him, yet he never showed it publicly, choosing instead to demonstrate constant self-control. In so doing, he gave to baseball and his country more than he had ever dreamed possible.

The Heart of a Champion maintains self-control even in personal attack:

What Robinson did for baseball still remains the greatest event in the history of the game. What he did for society as a whole remains even greater. As the person chosen to integrate baseball, Robinson's impact reached far beyond sport and was the key event to begin the change of the landscape of race in America. He could not have accomplished all he did without tremendous courage. He knew what he was going to experience, yet he still agreed to fill the role, understanding that it was his destiny. Because of that, Robinson soldiered on in the face of unthinkable opposition and hatred, knowing that he was called to a purpose greater than himself.

Courage has been described as knowing what is right and doing it anyway, and the right path to take is often the most difficult. Yet no great achievement in human existence was ever accomplished without the willingness of an individual to pay a significant price. Martin Luther, William Wallace, Rosa Parks, Abraham Lincoln, Martin Luther King, Jackie Robinson—*and Jesus Christ.* The willingness to pay a great price—to lay down one's very life—for the benefit of many: this is a demonstration of great moral courage. To what purpose is God calling you that will require great moral courage? Are you willing to pay the price? As difficult as it might be, are you willing to do it anyway?

> *"Have I not commanded you? Be strong and courageous.*
> *Do not be terrified; do not be discouraged, for the*
> *LORD your God will be with you wherever you go."*

—Joshua 1:9

"[Rodriguez'] message is extraordinary. Remember where you come from, give back to your community, pursue the highest standards of excellence."

—Donna Shalala,
President of the University of Miami

COMMITMENT:

A champion is committed to helping others.

Shortstop Alex Rodriguez is known by many as the top player in baseball today. He is a true superstar who has revolutionized his position and is considered the finest all-around shortstop in the history of the game. While most of the baseball media and fans seem to know him best as the man who signed a $252 million contract, to see Rodriguez simply in light of his financial status grossly underestimates this man's value.

He is one of the hardest-working athletes today, constantly applying himself to improve various aspects of his game. He is a leader both through word and example. He is an all-star, a home run record holder, and a team MVP. A-Rod, as he is known around the baseball world, is the national pastime's answer to Michael Jordan, Tiger Woods, and Jeff Gordon. Yet, above all of the accolades and titles, Rodriguez wants to be known as one more thing, a college graduate.

Following his historic 2002 season, A-Rod announced to the national press that he would begin pursuing a business degree from the University of Miami-Florida, beginning the process by taking correspondence classes. At the same time, he announced he was donating $3.9 million to the university's baseball program to create a scholarship at the Boys and Girls Club of America and to renovate the baseball field at Miami, renamed in his honor.

Both announcements tell much about him. His commitment to pursue his degree stems from a promise made in high school and is reinforced by his desire to set an example for young people. His charitable gift to the university is a clear sign of his unselfishness, confirming that his focus is not merely money. In both instances, his desire to impact the lives of children gives a glimpse of his desire to make a difference.

"It's always been my dream to earn a degree from the University of Miami," said Rodriguez, who specified his plans to major in business and minor in finance. "I'm not sure what I'd like to do with my degree, but this gives me a lot of options. I could see myself being a part owner of a team or possibly getting into the business world. But a degree gives me more of a chance to pursue something like that."

Rodriguez who hit .300 with 57 homers in 2002 at the age of twenty-seven was fulfilling a promise he had made to his mother that he would eventually go back and earn a degree after bypassing the opportunity coming out of high school. He was offered a baseball scholarship by the University of Miami upon graduating from Westminster Christian High School in Miami, but instead signed with the Seattle Mariners who made him the first selection in the 1993 draft. When negotiations with the Mariners broke down, on his mother's advice Alex headed for class at the Coral Gables campus. But just steps before he entered a classroom that morning, a Seattle scout stopped him. By the end of the day, A-Rod was a Mariner.

A decade later A-Rod has kept his promise to his mother by pursuing his degree and setting a remarkable example.

"His message is extraordinary," says Donna Shalala, President of the University of Miami. "Remember where you came from, give back to your community, pursue the highest standards of excellence."

The Heart of a Champion remains committed to people, principles, and promises:

Alex Rodriguez has spent many days being referred to as "Mr. 252," as in the $252 million contract he signed with the Texas Rangers in 2000. Yet Rodriguez is a man of deep substance, as both of his commitments to the University of Miami demonstrate. To pledge such a large amount of money to help in the formation of young lives is admirable. To act to obtain his college degree is perhaps a statement even more profound.

Surely he has the money to give, but the actual giving of a sum so large is extremely rare among today's athletes. But in getting his degree, Rodriguez is going beyond material sacrifice. The emphasis here is on honoring his word and setting an example for others. Our culture today lacks true promise keepers and men and women who care about teaching by example. In keeping his promise to his mother and determining that he can't encourage children to get an education if he has not done the same, A-Rod is putting all of himself "on the line" to show the way for others.

It is one thing to speak a good example, it is another to live that example. When we do this, we have entered an entirely different realm of modeling character. Words without actions are worthless. When our actions match our words, others notice and follow our example. Are you a person of your word? Check your actions for the answer.

> *The man of integrity walks securely, but he who takes crooked paths will be found out.*
>
> —Proverbs 10:9

" . . . pitching is more than going out there and throwing a baseball. It's going out there with a purpose of trying to keep your team in the game as long as you can, even when you don't have your best stuff."

LEADERSHIP:

A champion is a mentor.

O vercoming a very shaky start to his major league baseball career, Randy Johnson is firmly entrenched as one of the most dominant pitchers of this era. His performance earned him the Cy Young Award as his league's best pitcher in 1995, 1999, 2000, and 2001. His one-two punch combo of a blazing fastball and nasty slider has made hitters fear him. But Hall of Fame success seemed out of reach in Johnson's first years.

No one doubted that Johnson could intimidate hitters. After all, he was fast. And tall. At the start of his career, the 6-foot-10-inch left-hander used his height and a hint of wildness to his advantage. By the time his 98-mph heater left his hand, the batter felt it was already on top of him. But by Johnson's own admission, it took years of searching before he became a pitcher instead of a thrower.

Ironically, it was his boyhood hero and major league foe, Nolan Ryan, who played a key role in Johnson's coming-of-age process. During the 1992 season, Ryan's Texas Rangers and Johnson's Seattle Mariners were both out of play-off contention early, so Ryan thought nothing of helping an opposing pitcher—especially Johnson, in whom Ryan saw so much of himself.

Gene Clines, a Seattle coach at the time, asked Ryan to consider helping Johnson, who was struggling through an eleven-game stretch in which he'd gone 2-9 with a 5.63 ERA and tons of walks. Ryan invited Johnson to shadow him through a forty-five minute workout with pitching coach Tom House, hours before the game in the empty Seattle Kingdome. Then the men talked pitching. Whatever Ryan said worked. Johnson's next start was a 3-hit, 10-strikeout masterpiece against Kansas City. A month later he struck out 18 in 8 innings at Texas before taking himself out of the game. He was on his way.

Since the start of the 1993 season, Johnson has had Hall of Fame numbers: nearly 170 wins, three ERA titles, four 300-strikeout seasons, and Cy Young Awards in each league. He has gone from Seattle to Houston to Arizona in the high-stakes free-agent game; but through it all he has kept things in perspective in the midst of a marvelous career that almost never was, all because an opponent lent a hand to give Johnson a new perspective.

"He couldn't have been better," Johnson said. "He was very helpful, and I came away with a lot of confidence. For Nolan, I think it was his way of passing things on. It was very special for me . . . It helped me realize that pitching is more than going out there and throwing a baseball. It's going out there with a purpose of trying to keep your team in the game as long as you can, even when you don't have your best stuff.

"I can look you in the eye and tell you I have never enjoyed playing baseball more than I do now," Johnson says. "Not in Little League, not in high school, not in college. The word *potential* used to hang over me like a cloud. People would say, 'What kind of game are we going to get today?' Now I'm content."

"I was just trying to help a fellow pitcher, but my role wasn't that large," Ryan said. "Mostly when I'm asked to talk to other pitchers, it's like a five-minute conversation. They come with questions, but they have their own answers. They hear me, but they aren't listening. Randy was totally different. He truly wanted a different point of view."

The Heart of a Champion understands that sharing knowledge is a responsibility:

Nolan Ryan was pitted against Randy Johnson. Their teams were battling against each other in pursuit of a baseball championship. Yet Ryan understood that his responsibility went beyond the games his team played. He knew he had a responsibility in the game of baseball to impart what he had learned over the span of his illustrious career.

Ryan had been blessed, and he needed to pass that blessing on. Transferring his knowledge to Johnson was good for the game. Think of what Ryan has meant to baseball and its fans in pouring his experience into Johnson. Johnson has become one of the most dominant pitchers in the history of baseball, winning five Cy Young Awards through 2002. In many ways Ryan replicated himself in Johnson. It is nearly certain: without Ryan's influence, the game never would have enjoyed the marvel that is Johnson.

As Christians, we have been blessed with so much. What we do with that is the measure of the character of Christ in us. During Jesus' time with His disciples, He was constantly mentoring them, teaching them, and showing them the way in which they should live. His purpose was not merely to give them answers but also to bring them to a place where they could take what He had imparted and *live* it. It is true that character is "caught," and others must see it lived in us in order to embrace it for themselves.

It is your responsibility as a believer in Christ to mentor others. Let them see your life. Tell them, and *show* them how you do it. Let them glean from your experience. Replicate the good that has been developed in you. Pass it on. This is the pattern that Christ set. So whom are you mentoring?

The things you have heard me say in the presence
of many witnesses entrust to reliable men
who will also be qualified to teach others.

—2 Timothy 2:2

Profile of NOLAN RYAN

"My job is to give my team a chance to win."

—Baseball Almanac

EXCELLENCE:

Champions build toward excellence from wherever they start.

Nolan Ryan's credentials are familiar to those who followed his remarkable career with the New York Mets, California Angels, Houston Astros, and Texas Rangers. He is baseball's all-time record holder with 5,714 career strikeouts and 7 no-hitters. With his 324 career victories, he is tied for 12th all time. He owns 53 major league records and was an amazing model of physical prowess over an extended period. Also, he was a shining example of character, never complaining while performing for lowly teams.

It was in high school that Ryan first gained a dedication to excellence. As a senior, Ryan completely dominated Gulf Coast baseball, posting a record of 19-3 and carrying the Alvin Yellow Jackets to the Texas high school state finals in Austin. Over the 32-game season in the spring of 1965, Ryan pitched in 27 of the games, started 20, and finished the year with 12 complete games, 211 strikeouts, and only 61 walks.

Alvin head coach, Jim Watson, and players from the 1965 team described Ryan's senior year performance as the team's "wheel horse"—the horse closest to the wagon that pulls the heaviest share of the load. He demonstrated a capacity for pitching that few would have ever tried. On March 25, 1965, Ryan pitched 3 innings of relief, giving up 1 run and striking out 5. That same night he started another game, pitching 5 innings, while giving up just 1 hit and striking out 10 in a 9-2 victory. On April 1 and 3, in a space of forty-eight hours, Ryan pitched back-to-back complete game victories.

Heading into the postseason, he got better. Ryan pitched a no-hitter against Brenham High on June 10, striking out 12. Five days later, in the state semifinals he threw a two-hit shutout against Snyder High, striking out 9. The speed of his fastball and his intimidation made him almost unstoppable.

Some of the stories told of Ryan's senior year are more memorable than his pitching statistics. After a bout of wildness in the first inning of a March 20 game against Deer Park, during which Ryan cracked the batting helmet of the leadoff hitter and then hit and broke the next batter's arm, the third hitter decided he had seen enough and refused to enter the batter's box. His coach finally shamed him into an at bat that produced the season's quickest three-pitch strikeout. In the June 10 regional playoff against Brenham, Ryan's inside fastballs kept causing opposing hitters' bats to break.

But Ryan's high school heat sawed off more than bats. His catcher's hands deteriorated as well. One season, Alvin catcher Jerry Spinks observed a small tear in his mitt, which quickly developed into a sizable hole, caused by the force of Ryan's fastball. He compared the sound of Nolan's heater hitting the glove to a "muffled rifle shot." The seemingly bullet-holed mitt caused repercussions: "No matter how much padding I put in my glove," Spinks said, "as each game wore on, I had fewer fingers on my left hand capable of gripping a bat."

When young major league baseball scout Red Murff, working for the New York Mets, first caught a glimpse of Ryan, he knew he had stumbled onto someone special.

"He wound up again and threw another pitch that looked like it had come from a rocket launcher, this time on the outside corner of the plate for another strike," Murff would relate later in his book *The Scout.* "You could hear it sizzle like a thick slab of ham frying on a red-hot griddle as it roared toward the plate.

"That God had richly blessed this young man was blatantly obvious. That fastball of his was unbelievable. It was the fastest I'd ever seen anywhere. . . . And it had life. It jumped off his hand and appeared to hop as it hurtled toward home plate."

A year and a half later the Mets drafted Ryan in the eighth round of the 1965 amateur draft, on Murff's recommendation. Ryan posted a 17-2 record that first season in the minors before making his major league debut. And, as is commonly said, the rest is history.

The legend of the Ryan Express began in a small Texas town, when a young, skinny kid with a once-in-a-lifetime arm, set out to become the best pitcher baseball had ever seen. He dedicated himself to never being outworked, and he never was. Because of that, he was a physical marvel, with his fastball terrorizing hitters well into his forties. From the small beginnings, the legend would grow to Hall of Fame proportions.

The Heart of a Champion appreciates the past:

Nolan Ryan grew up in a small town in Texas. He was a skinny kid with a live arm that had trouble finding the strike zone. Yet he never let what he was or where he came from become a deterrent to where he was going. His commitment to excellence and dedication to reaching his destiny overrode any obstacle his circumstances presented.

When you look back at your past, what do you see? Do you remember what you didn't have? Or do you look back with a grateful heart at what God was building into you during those days? Surely baseball scouts must have asked the question, "Can anything good come out of Alvin, Texas?" And, "This is just a skinny kid from nowhere—how could he amount to anything?" Similar remarks were made about Jesus, yet He never let it become an issue or deter Him from His destiny. He simply followed the Father's plan for Him and reached His destiny. No matter what your past, it should not hinder you from fulfilling your destiny. Simply follow the Father's plan, and leave the past in His hands.

Philip found Nathanael and told him, "We have found the one Moses wrote about in the Law, and about whom the prophets also wrote—Jesus of Nazareth, the son of Joseph."

"Nazareth! Can anything good come from there?" Nathanael asked. "Come and see," said Phillip.

—John 1:45-46

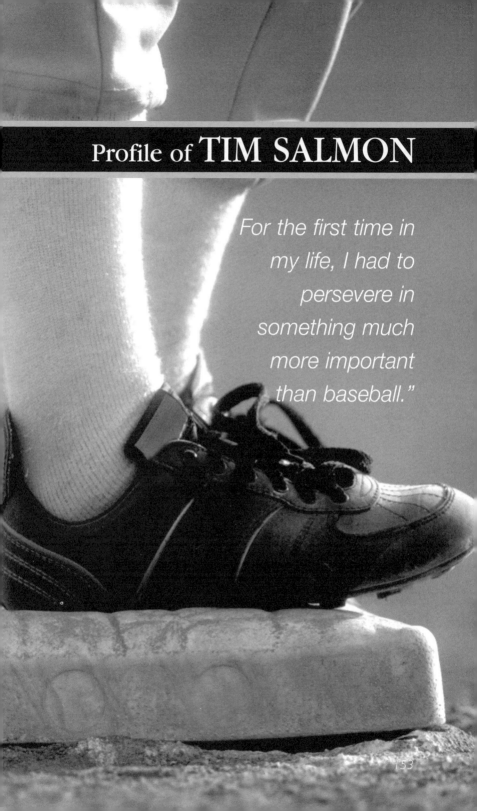

Profile of TIM SALMON

For the first time in my life, I had to persevere in something much more important than baseball."

PERSEVERANCE:

A champion is single-minded in purpose.

t was 1997 and the Anaheim Angels' Tim Salmon was having another outstanding year at the plate. He was leading Anaheim in home runs and RBIs. His average was hovering around .300, and he had further established himself as one of the top right fielders in all of baseball. Yet all was not well.

The 1997 season did not begin well for Tim Salmon. It wasn't a slump at the plate that bothered him. Rather, it was learning that spring that his wife, Marci, had cancer. The young father of two young children now had to balance his wife's illness with his baseball career during those early months of the season.

"At the start of the season she had some swollen glands," Salmon said of his wife. "This was in April. They checked them out, and she had a biopsy. We then found out it was thyroid cancer. We took her to surgery shortly thereafter.

"There were a couple of days where, like when I first found out, the emotion on the field wasn't there, the intensity wasn't there."

In 19 games from May 12 to June 3 of 1997, Salmon suffered the worst slump of his career, hitting .203 with 1 home run and 17 strikeouts.

"Mentally I felt I was separating [my wife's illness and my playing], but my performance sure didn't show it," he said. "My swing was terrible, and subconsciously I was letting the situation get to me."

Throughout that difficult period Salmon spoke regularly to Anaheim hitting instructor Rod Carew, who had lost his daughter Michelle to leukemia.

In a four-hour operation in June of 1997, Marci's thyroid was removed. In the first 18 games after the surgery, a relieved Salmon hit .419 with 5 home runs and 19 RBIs.

"It just so happened that when things kind of got settled at home, and we found out . . . and that everything was getting taken care of, I just started warming up with the bat," Salmon says.

"It makes you realize how meaningless a batting slump is compared to the possibility of losing a spouse. I think I'm a little more mellow now and funneling my intensity better. It definitely puts things in perspective."

On January 22, 1998, the Salmons made the trek back to Anaheim from their home in Phoenix for the six-month checkup and radiation scan. The news was an answer to their prayer.

"Everything is perfect," Marci says. "It was a huge relief. It surprised me how good it felt. Now we can just close the book on this and go on."

Going on for Tim meant battering American League pitchers, which he has consistently done since Marci's surgery. He is continually among the American league's leaders in home runs, RBIs, and run production, all the while playing stellar defense. More than that, he has gained a new appreciation for his wife and says God opened his eyes to the joy that's in his life.

"I'm thankful that I had the opportunity to have my eyes opened and be enlightened as to the joy that is around me and that maybe I take for granted," Tim says. "I've had to persevere in my life, but it's always applied to baseball. For the first time in my life, I had to persevere in something much more important than baseball. That's what this whole spiritual journey is about—growing in our faith and being more Christ-like every day."

The heart of a champion never gives up:

Just as with his batting slumps, Tim Salmon was faced with something he could not cure on his own, when his wife discovered she had cancer. Salmon realized that some things are too big for us to take care of or control. So he learned to give his worries—about his wife's health and his own performance—over to God. Therein, he found peace.

We are told in God's Word to "cast" our cares upon Jesus. The word cast here means to throw, or to cast as if casting a fishing line. We are told to cast them all. Jesus is so ready to take your cares, worries, and anxieties—every single one of them. Why? Because He cares for you. In other words, you are the object of His care, and because of that, He wants to lift the burden of worry and anxiety from you and give you peace. But it is up to us to give those anxieties over to Him. Will you throw them all at the feet of the Savior?

Cast all your anxiety on him because He cares for you.

—1 Peter 5:7

"Don't ever become complacent. That's been my motto in baseball and no matter where I'm at, I'm always trying to improve what I'm doing."

CONVICTION:

A champion makes choices based on what is right.

After winning the 1996 Cy Young Award and becoming the winningest post-season, starting pitcher in baseball history, the Atlanta Braves John Smoltz was recognized as one of baseball's finest starters—when he stayed healthy.

Arm problems plagued Smoltz in 1994, 1998, and 2000, nearly bringing a premature end to a brilliant career. After blowing out his elbow for the third time, Smoltz underwent reconstructive surgery, known in baseball circles as "Tommy John" surgery, in March 2000. His future was uncertain. After sitting out fourteen months, Smoltz returned to the Braves rotation in 2001. But his elbow could not handle the strain, and after just twenty-five innings, he was once again shut down for the season in June.

Smoltz had just twenty-five innings and as many trips to the disabled list and 2 victories to show for two seasons. He was at a career crossroads. Braves brass felt that when Smoltz came back at the end of the 2001 season, the best chance of maximizing his health would be to put him in the bull pen and make him the team's closer. Smoltz agreed it would be the best way to work him back into his former role. So over the final two months of the 2001 season, Smoltz relieved Braves management by becoming a dominant closer, saving ten of eleven games in which he pitched. The future suddenly held promise.

With his contract up in the off-season, Smoltz fielded offers from a number of teams promising to return him to the starting rotation. The Braves wanted him to stay in Atlanta, but now as the permanent closer. Along with the job change, Atlanta offered him less money than the other suitors. In the end, he chose home, the role change, and less money. It was a refreshing display of humility, loyalty, and priority from a bona fide star.

"It was the most complicated and hardest decision I've ever had to make," Smoltz says. "I talked with a lot of friends. I consulted my family. I prayed about it. All of the answers that I got led toward staying here. Sure there was more money; and there were more situations that on the outside, the world looks at like, 'You fool!' But I've never chased the money, and I've never been a person that would make my decisions solely on the world's view or the easy way out.

"It was a tough decision. Family had a lot to do with it as well as all the community work, charity work. I'm involved in a Christian school, and that was a big part of it. I think people think that the [money] is the only issue that matters and that could get you happiness, and it doesn't work that way. I was flattered and enjoyed the opportunity of seeking somebody else if it didn't work out here, but I'm glad it did."

The "starter turned closer" was dominant in his first full season in that role in 2002. Smoltz set a national league record by converting 55 saves, just 2 shy of the major league mark. He again made the all-star team and was a runner-up for the Cy Young Award. In 80 innings, he allowed only 59 hits and posted 85 strikeouts. He finished the season with a 3 and 2 record and a 3.25 ERA. Over the final two-thirds of the season, as he settled into his role, he was nearly unhittable.

At age thirty-four, a star was reborn, as was a career.

"I'm happy," says Smoltz. "I've always wanted to end my career in Atlanta Braves, and I have that opportunity; and my family's happy, and I hope the Braves are happy."

In this case, "happy" would be an understatement.

The Heart of a Champion recognizes that the most profitable things are not always measured in dollars.

John Smoltz had a number of baseball general managers throwing out very large salary figures in their attempts to lure him to their teams for 2002. For a professional athlete, those numbers and the promise of a starting pitcher position were enticing. But when it came down to decision time, Smoltz knew his choice was based on one thing only: What was the best plan for his family and his life beyond? To him, staying in Atlanta was the clear answer. He chose substance over sizzle, contentment over conjecture, and peace of mind over money.

Conviction is defined as "the state of being convinced; a strong belief." Our convictions, or strong beliefs, are the guidelines by which we make choices. Critical thinking requires a set of convictions from which to act. Without conviction, it is impossible to take a stand and hold it. In a culture that rarely encourages conviction, however, it is a true statement that if we don't stand for something, we will fall for anything. Our culture has produced emotional uncertainty and psychological confusion. It needs to see men and women of conviction who will not merely speak their strong beliefs but actually live them out. People around you don't want to hear it as much as they would desperately like to *see* one who truly lives what he believes.

> *Do not merely listen to the word, and*
> *so deceive yourselves. Do what it says.*
>
> —James 1:22

COMMITMENT:

A champion stays focused.

After finishing the 2001 season with great success as the Atlanta Braves closer, many expected Smoltz to make the full-time transition from starter to reliever quickly and easily. Smoltz says that after eleven years as a starting pitcher in the major leagues, the change was more difficult than he had expected.

"I don't think I could ever explain how difficult it was to make the transition," he says. "I wasn't ready coming out of spring training. I didn't throw at all off-season, and everyone expected me to be so dominant. That's not to mention that the first few weeks of the season we were terrible, and I'm introducing myself to the role."

Smoltz made it *look* easy. His 55 saves were not only a national league record but just two away from the major league mark. The last half of the season he was nearly flawless. Just one other pitcher in baseball history had made such a successful transition from starter to closer, Oakland's Dennis Eckersley. Why was Smoltz able to accomplish the move? Those who know him say the answer is easy.

"He's one of the most competitive people I've met in forty-three years in the game," said Atlanta's bull pen coach Bobby Dews of his pitcher during the 2002 season.

Says Smoltz: "I really believe it started from that age of seven years old, and I haven't lost that spirit of competition of being at my best. I love to compete. I want to be at that pinnacle of what we do. I don't play just for numbers or records. I want to be able to compete at the highest level to be a world champion. And the one thing that drives me I really believe is an inner desire. It's nothing that's been force-fed. I don't play for the money. That wasn't the reason that it attracted me. And that's the reason I'm still able to play at this age."

That competitive spirit was birthed when Smoltz traded his accordion for a bat and glove. Smoltz learned to play the accordion at age four and became a prodigy, winning contests as far away as Chicago. But once he discovered baseball, the accordion was rarely heard again.

"At the age of seven for whatever reason, that was in my heart—to be a major league baseball player," Smoltz remembers. "I asked my parents if I could quit playing [the accordion] and pursue baseball. I was fortunate enough that they allowed me to pursue a dream that I'm sure at that age didn't seem real realistic. It became my focus. In everything that I did, I strived towards making it in the major leagues.

"My mom said, 'That's great, but you need something to fall back on.'

"I told her, 'A gas station attendant looks pretty fun.'

"She said, 'Well, don't tell your dad.'"

Smoltz decided to forgo the gas station. At sixteen, after serving up three home runs in a national amateur tournament, he taped a strike zone on the back of the house in Lansing, Michigan, and spent hours pitching at the makeshift zone. Baseball consumed him. As a high school senior, he even skipped the homecoming dance to watch the Detroit Tigers play in the World Series. "I never had any other interests," Smoltz admits.

Even today, as one of the top performers in the game, he continues to approach his job with similar zeal. Smoltz says, "Don't ever become complacent. That's been my motto in baseball; and no matter where I'm at, I'm always trying to improve what I'm doing."

The Heart of a Champion remains single-minded and focused on the purposes of God:

John Smoltz had a difficult task in 2002. While at a casual glance to transition from a starting pitcher to a closer would seem an easy transition, the opposite is true. Such a change means completely different regimens physically and emotionally. Yet when Smoltz decided he would make the change, he didn't vacillate. He aimed every effort at succeeding in that new role. He did not rely on his talent but took every necessary step to equip himself to see maximum results. He put the past behind him and set his sights on the future. He did the same at age seven—when he put down the accordion, he put it down for good.

So often we live in the past—all of the "has beens," "could have beens," and "should have beens" of our experience. Our glance at the past has a tendency to affect our present, as we ponder alternative routes in life rather than the one God has placed before us. It is a constant struggle to insist on our own way. Yet God tells us this is double-minded, and the double-minded can expect to receive nothing. What road has God placed before you? Identify it, and "set your face like flint" toward it. Embrace that path, and take every step to produce the maximum results God desires. Whatever the accordion represents in your life, lay it down. Give your all to what God has placed in your hands.

But when he asks, he must believe and not doubt, because he who doubts is like a wave of the sea, blown and tossed by the wind. That man should not think he will receive anything from the Lord; he is a double-minded man, unstable in all he does.

—James 1:6-8

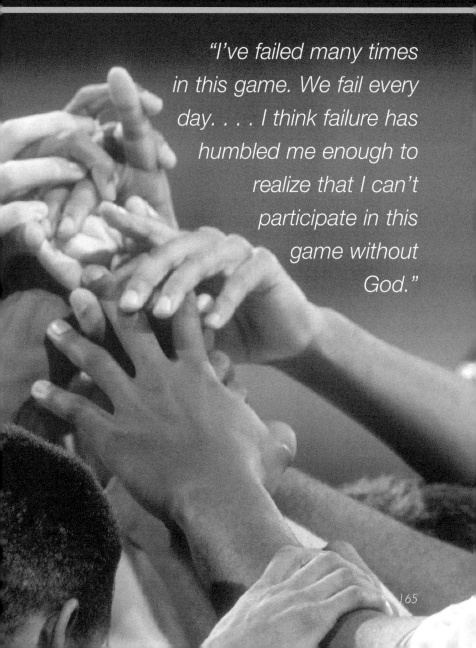

Profile of STEVE SPARKS

"I've failed many times in this game. We fail every day. . . . I think failure has humbled me enough to realize that I can't participate in this game without God."

CONTENTMENT:

Champions use the gifts they've been given.

F ew things in baseball are more humbling to a major league
batter than being retired by a pitcher who throws a ball 50
mph. But if those hitters are facing veteran knuckleball
pitcher Steve Sparks, this is common.

Sparks, who has pitched with the Milwaukee Brewers, Anaheim
Angels, and Detroit Tigers during his career, is a vanishing breed.
Back in the middle of the last century, knuckleball pitchers were
not uncommon on a number of major league rosters. But in the
new millennium, Sparks is one of only two true knuckleball spe-
cialists to have pitched regularly on any big league team.

"The biggest thing about a knuckleball is it's hard to throw for
strikes," says Sparks. "The one thing that I've learned is that I have
to stay real patient with it and just realize that I am, maybe, just one
pitch—one good knuckleball—away from a double play. I have to
stick with it."

Sparks's approach has allowed him to show that a knuckleballer
can still succeed in the majors. He recorded 14 wins for the Tigers
in 2001, finished among the American league leaders in ERA and
complete games, and was selected as the Tigers Player of the Year
by the Detroit area chapter of the professional baseball writers. It
was the highlight of an interesting journey.

Profile of Steve Sparks

That journey began in 1987 when he joined the Brewers organization out of Sam Houston State College (Texas). After four years without getting past Double A, Brewers' brass suggested in 1991 that Sparks learn the knuckler. "I was a little disappointed," he says. "I thought my stuff was good enough. But looking back, it probably wasn't."

Learning the pitch wasn't easy because few coaches can teach it. So one of the first things Sparks did was call Los Angeles Dodgers knuckleball pitcher Tom Candiotti. The two flutter ballers spoke a few times by phone; and Sparks went to a Dodgers game to visit with Candiotti in person, watch him pitch, and learn more. Sparks was on his way.

He was close to sticking at the big league level with Milwaukee in 1994, but a few weeks before spring training camp broke the team was visited by a group of motivational speakers called Radical Reality. Members of the group were bending iron bars, ripping phone books in half, and exhibiting other similar feats of strength. The next day Sparks and a few teammates tried the phone-book feat with the Phoenix Yellow Pages. Sparks had the book almost torn in half when he dislocated his left shoulder. Out for several weeks with the injury, he ended up not getting out of Triple A that year. The incident was written up in *Sports Illustrated* and carried in newspapers across the country. The story still has life.

"To this day, going into Boston and New York, [the media gets] such a kick out of the story that I sign telephone books there and still am able to put a scripture verse underneath," he says.

Sparks finally reached the majors in 1995, where he has stayed, but not without challenges, not the least of which remains the constant battle to be successful at getting major league hitters out, using a 50-mph floater.

"I've failed many times in this game. We fail every day," he says. "I think maybe just because this game is so humbling that you realize what's important and who is important. I think failure has humbled me enough to realize that I can't participate in this game without God."

The Heart of a Champion appreciates the uniqueness of gifts:

When he began his professional baseball career, Steve Sparks wanted to be like any other successful pitcher, rely on his fastball, mix in a breaking pitch and an off-speed pitch to keep the batters off balance, throw hard, move the ball around the strike zone, and hit the target. About the only one of those goals he achieves today is to move the ball around—sometimes to the point that he doesn't know where it will end up. His use of his individual talents is clearly unconventional, yet Sparks says he is using his talents in the most effective manner. In his case, being different has brought success that, for Sparks, conformity would not.

It is common to wonder why we are not equipped like others. Yet God marks creation by an amazing pattern of uniqueness. No two created things are exactly alike—from snowflakes to humans. You have been created by God to be unlike anyone else, with your own unique gifts. When young David challenged Goliath, he had a choice to use Saul's armor or a sling and some rocks—the weapons that were familiar to him. Just as David chose instead to use his own weapons, you too have been created to use the gifts God has given you to fulfill your destiny.

> *Then Saul dressed David in his own tunic. He put*
> *a coat of armor on him and a bronze helmet*
> *on his head. David fastened on his sword over the*
> *tunic and tried walking around, because he was not*
> *used to them. "I cannot go in these," he said to Saul,*
> *"because I am not used to them." So he took them off.*
> *Then he . . . chose five smooth stones . . . and, with*
> *his sling in his hand, approached the Philistine.*
>
> —1 Samuel 17:38-40

PREPARATION:

A champion prepares for success.

For knuckleball pitcher Steve Sparks, preparing to pitch in a game is every bit as important as the actual game performance. If Sparks misses out on even a small element of his routine, it can mean disaster come game time. First, unlike most big league pitchers, Sparks throws often in between starts. While other pitchers want to rest their arms to regain strength on their off days, Sparks never wants his arm to get too strong. Too much arm strength means too much velocity, resulting in too much rotation on the ball upon release. This is bad because then the knuckler will not knuckle.

"When you're not actually taking the spin off the ball, which is what I'm supposed to do," says Sparks, "then it's really easy to hit."

And at all times when he throws, the goal is again a bit different from other pitchers. "I have to be really precise all of the time, even playing catch with my mechanics," Sparks says. "If I have a mechanical flaw, it's going to be magnified when I pitch because it [the ball] is coming so slowly. If it starts missing the mark, then it's going to miss the strike zone altogether. If I start getting lazy with some of my mechanics, I'm afraid it will carry over into the game. So I'm working on my mechanics constantly."

When everything comes together on the mound, Sparks' knuckler appears to dip, dance, swirl, and float. For the batter, it is like playing a classic parlor game of "now you see it, now you don't." Sometimes even Sparks is unsure where a given pitch will end up.

"If I do throw a good knuckleball, and it happens to be windy, it's virtually impossible for anybody to catch cleanly every pitch of the game. They probably will get hit on the face mask once or twice. . . . If it's on TV, it's a little embarrassing."

Sparks' tools of the trade can also be a bit embarrassing, but a necessary part of the preparation for a knuckleball pitcher. The most important elements in Sparks' locker are simple, a fingernail file and clippers. Sparks can't throw the knuckleball well without a good manicure. Since strong fingernails on the index and middle fingers are key to a successful knuckler, Sparks may be one of the only players in baseball who spends considerable time grooming his nails.

"You have to worry about getting them chipped a lot," he says. "It's my bread and butter, so I have to protect them. A lot of times I will eat with just my other two fingers. I keep a gel over them so it keeps them a little thicker, and I take gelatin capsules from time to time if I feel like they're getting a little thinner. I don't do any [grooming] in front of the guys . . . and I don't do it in front of my kids, either."

Few pitchers will leave batters grumbling and shaking their heads as much as Sparks, as they head back to the dugout after failing to make contact with his tantalizingly slow floaters. Should the ball spin too much, however, it will not move at all. Sparks knows all too well what major league hitters do to slow pitches that are completely straight—he has watched many long home runs on nights when the ball has not danced as desired. Few knuckleball pitchers have sustained success at the big league level over the last decade. Still, Sparks continues to tempt the percentages.

"You have to be a little goofy to throw a 50-mph pitch to these guys," says Sparks. "I can't go out there and participate without God. That gives you the confidence if you can just go out there and do your best no matter what happens."

The Heart of a Champion knows that the will to prepare is as crucial as the will to win:

Steve Sparks' method of preparation is a bit different than that of his peers, yet he is equally as committed. To Sparks, diligent preparation means taking care of little things. It is hard to imagine a professional athlete being concerned with the care of his fingernails, but Sparks knows that his nails are his livelihood. So he goes to great lengths with their upkeep. His throwing mechanics also require intense attention to detail. Without care for the most minute details, he knows he cannot expect success.

A well-known coach once said, "The will to prepare to win is more important than the will to win." This is true of athletes, as well as those in business, or in just about any walk of life. How will we respond when decisive moments come, if we have not prepared before they arrive? Just as the world's finest athletes don't just show up and play, we cannot hope to find success by just arriving at our destiny and hoping we will be able to react or respond appropriately. Jesus was not surprised when He was taken to the Cross. Rather, He knew it was to come and had prepared for His destiny. We also must do all of the things—both little and big—to prepare for our moment of destiny.

"Be dressed ready for service and keep your lamps
burning. . . . It will be good for those servants whose
master finds them watching when he comes. . . .
You also must be ready, because the Son of Man will
come at an hour when you do not expect him."

—Luke 12:35,37,40

Profile of MIKE SWEENEY

"I had this vivid picture in my head of a tandem bicycle, and it represented my life. I was trying to be on the front seat steering my way and have the Lord jump on the back seat and help me pedal. It became obvious to me that the roles had to be reversed."

HUMILITY:

Champions realize they cannot succeed in their own strength.

Mike Sweeney is a humble California native who almost seems too good to be true and too good to be unknown. Still, in his first four full seasons as the Kansas City Royals starting first baseman, he has put up MVP-type numbers without drawing much notice.

In the 1999 season, his first as a starter, Sweeney hit .322 with 22 home runs, 102 RBIs. He followed that in 2000 by hitting .333 with 29 homers and a team record 144 RBIs, to go along with 206 hits and 105 runs scored. It was the first time any American League player had hit over .330 with 200 hits and 140 RBIs since Al Rosen accomplished the feat in 1953. Sweeney didn't let up in 2001 or 2002, producing seasons of .304, 29, 99 in 2001; and .340, 24, 86 in 2002, when he narrowly missed winning the American League batting title. Yet outside of Kansas City, who knows about Mike Sweeney?

Opponents do. Says former A's manager, Art Howe, "He has no apparent weakness at the plate. He can hit the fastball, the off-speed pitch, and the slider. What do you do with a guy like that?"

That's what American League managers have been asking themselves since Sweeney broke into the lineup in 1999. Prior to that, even Royals management didn't really know who he was. From

1995 when he was first called up to big leagues, through 1997, Sweeney was labeled as a decent-hit, no-field catcher. During that time, the Royals were managed by Bob Boone, a former all-star catcher who likes his catchers short and blocky, not rangy and athletic like the 6-foot-3-inch, 225-pound Sweeney. When Sweeney couldn't adapt to what Boone wanted, observers say Boone gave up on him, which hindered Sweeney's progress. Still, Sweeney refuses to be critical of his former manager.

"Mike was a pretty good catcher," says Sal Fasano, a former team-mate and catcher who played with the Royals from 1996 to 1999, "but he didn't have that body type. I don't think Boonie meant to hurt him, but he tried changing Mike, and it didn't work. After playing the position his whole life, they told Mike he couldn't catch. How would you feel?"

Low is how Sweeney felt. His career was at a crossroads prior to the 1999 season. Each day he was hit with the latest trade rumors, hearing daily that he was headed to some other team. Then Royals Executive Vice President Herk Robinson says of that time, "I'm not sure who's dumber, us for trying to trade Mike, or other teams for not taking him."

"I kept looking at myself saying, *You know what? I am a good athlete. I am a good ballplayer. I shouldn't be traded.* I was trying to do everything on my own."

In 1998 Tony Muser took over for Boone. He too had little regard for Sweeney's catching skills and told Sweeney he had no future in that position with the team. So on Ash Wednesday, two days before he was to leave for spring training in 1999, a discouraged Sweeney worked out at a gym and then drove to the Church of the Nativity where he attends. Tired and drained, he entered the sanctuary wearing sweats and running shoes. A service was underway, so Sweeney quietly found a place in the back of the church and dropped to his knees. He began to weep and pray.

"I had this vivid picture in my head of a tandem bicycle, and it represented my life," he recalls. "I was trying to be on the front seat steering my way and have the Lord jump on the back seat and help me pedal. It became obvious to me that the roles had to be reversed."

As he prayed, the image changed. Jesus was on the front seat, holding the handlebars. "I submitted that area of my life to Jesus Christ and said, 'Lord I do not know where I am going, but I cannot do this without You. You get on the front seat and steer my path. I will get on the back seat and pedal my heart out for You. Lord, there are six weeks until Opening Day. I don't know where I'm going, I don't know what city I'll end up in, but I know that You control my life and as long as I'm on the back seat peddling, everything will work out. No matter where I am, I will get on my knees and praise You.'"

The next day, still amidst swirling trade rumors, Sweeney was at peace. He reported to camp renewed, hit .361 in the spring, and made the team as the third-string catcher. "I didn't have a plan for Mike," says Muser of the time.

That changed in May, when first baseman Jeff King retired. In a team meeting, Muser asked if anyone had experience playing first base. Sweeney, who had played two games at first in Little League, raised his hand. He was on his way to finding his place in the game.

"It was the first time in my life that I had peace and joy in baseball—and freedom," he says. "And that is the big reason why I had success that year. For the first time, I let down the pride and selfishness in my life and said, 'I cannot do this on my own. Take away my strength and give me Yours.' For the first time in my life I had freedom and peace about playing the game of baseball."

The Heart of a Champion understands that true strength is found in release:

Mike Sweeney found himself in a difficult spot. He felt that he was talented enough to play regularly at the major league level, yet the Royals made it clear that he had no future with them as a catcher. What did he do? He gave up. Not in the practical sense, but in the sense of control of his life. Sweeney still dedicated himself to working hard to improve, but in his heart, he released control of his life and destiny to God. When he did this, he was able to perform without self-imposed pressure and eventually found freedom, peace, and joy—and great success.

Mike Sweeney came to a crossroads in his life that we all must face. It is perhaps the most difficult crucible of our human experience, to confront the choice to give up control of our own lives, to lay down our lives. Doing so is contrary to our natural desires, yet it is a must if we are to ever truly find peace. We cannot control our own destiny. In our efforts to do so, we burn out, walk out, or tune out. We become frustrated, cynical, and defeated. God wants to carry the burden of our future. He wants to lead the way to our destiny. Will you let Him? Are you willing to give up control of your life and let God lead the way?

The Lord is my shepherd, I shall not be in want.
He makes me lie down in green pastures, he leads me
beside quiet waters, he restores my soul. He guides
me in paths of righteousness for his name's sake.

—Psalm 23:1-3

GOODNESS:

A champion is a good example.

Mike Sweeney's father, Mike Sr., says he always knew that his son would be a ballplayer. He just didn't know he would turn out to be such a fine man.

When Mike was born six weeks prematurely, his father, a former minor league outfielder in the California Angels system in the early 1970s, placed a tiny plastic bat in the incubator as a hopeful sign of what was to come. After a week in the hospital, Sweeney's parents brought him home, but later that day he stopped breathing and turned blue. They rushed him back to the University of California Irvine Medical Center in Orange County, where Mike was revived. He remained in the hospital for a month. Perhaps it was just such a start that has molded Sweeney into a patient and compassionate human being. A clear understanding of how fragile life can be has inspired Mike to use his platform in baseball to influence others.

"I know through baseball we have been put on a platform, and people look up to us because of the uniform we wear on our back," Sweeney says. "I take the responsibility to be a good role model and setting an example not only to the guys on my team but also to the fans and people who watch us and my family. I definitely need to set a good example."

Throughout baseball, Sweeney is known for the example he has set. On the field, he is a tireless worker. Even after four straight seasons of hitting .300, and three selections to the all-star team, he continually strives to improve. Many off-seasons have seen him return home to Southern California for extended visits with his parents. Those trips inevitably find Mike and his dad down at Westwind Park, where Mike starred as a Little Leaguer. For hours at a time, his father has hit grounder after grounder to Mike at first base—thousands of balls every day, day after day. The converted catcher is determined to become a stellar glove man at first base. "I believe Mikey will win a Gold Glove one day," says his father. "Anything he's ever wanted to do, he's done. He wants to be a great first baseman."

More importantly, he wants to be a great person. Former Royals General Manager Herk Robinson calls him "one of the best humans you'll meet." Bob Beck, Sweeney's coach at Ontario High remembers how Sweeney had a soft spot for handicapped children in the area. "He would carry them around on his back, just to be good to them. You don't see that from people, not to mention high schoolers."

Jim Lachimia, Royals senior director of communications, remembers the night following the 1999 season when his father suffered a stroke. "The next morning I checked my voice mail, and there was a call from Mike. He left me the most touching message: 'Jim, I heard about your father. I want you to know last night I got on my knees and prayed for you and your dad.' It's not a front; Mike cares about people."

"Some people jokingly call me one of the nicest guys in baseball," says Sweeney, aware of the stereotype of athletes of faith. "I don't look at it as being soft. I look at it as love, whether it's going up to another guy on another team and giving him a hug, or a guy on your own team—just sharing encouragement in the locker room—I think that makes me a team player. Where that stems from? My faith in Jesus Christ."

Jeremy Giambi, who played with Kansas City during the 1999 season, received a call from Sweeney hours after being called up from the minors. "He said, 'Hey, why don't you live at my house for the rest of the season?' So I did. There are people with big hearts, and then there's Mike. His heart is the biggest."

"I look at my profession as a challenge," says Sweeney. "I want to be a light in this dark generation. . . . Rather than going into the darkness and being dark, I am going to try to be a light and shine in the darkness."

Sweeney's dad remembers one occasion after another when he has done just that, helping disabled people cross the street, sending Royals T-shirts and gloves and shoes to Beck and the Ontario High team, traveling to Germany after the 1999 season to share his faith in baseball clinics, and never turning down an opportunity to speak to youth groups. "My son is my role model," he says. "He doesn't need baseball so much as baseball needs him. He makes me extremely proud."

"Success—no matter what I do in life, whether I play first base for the Kansas City Royals or be a role model, or help out at a youth group—is doing the best I can, in mind and strength, to be an example of Jesus Christ. That is success in my eyes."

The Heart of a Champion is willing to set an example of character:

Mike Sweeney feels a sense of responsibility to be a good example for others. Not because he is a major league baseball player but because he is a human being. It is Sweeney's conviction that everyone should positively affect the lives of others. It is his desire to model Christ in all he does and have an impact on humanity. This is an easy thing for many athletes to say but more challenging for them to actually accomplish. Sweeney has made it his life's mission. His effectiveness in doing so is his measuring stick for personal success.

How do you measure success? Mike Sweeney's guide is how brightly his "light" shines in a dark world. How are you doing with your "light"? The temptation for the person of faith is to surround oneself in a comfortable environment. Our faith is displayed in our circles of faith, but work is work. When Jesus told us that we are the "light of the world," He meant it. He wanted us to understand that we have something the world desperately needs. But light can only be effective light when it is employed in darkness. In a room full of lights, one more light makes little difference. But in a dark room it can be crucial.

When we spend all our time shining in our circles of faith, we make little appreciable difference. When we shine in our dark world, we have an opportunity to see incredible change. Where are you shining your light? How are you affecting the culture? You are the light of the world. Let it shine.

"You are the light of the world. . . . let your light shine before men, that they may see your good deeds and praise your Father in heaven."

—Matthew 5:14,16

"Fame is fleeting, but the impact you make in the lives of others, to me, has eternal value."

COMPASSION:

A champion is quick to give to others.

In 1998 Dave Valle, who spent thirteen seasons as a catcher for Seattle, Boston, Milwaukee, and Texas, was sitting alone in a hotel room. A simple truth overwhelmed him—he would rather be home with his family and investing his time in people who needed him more than minor league pitchers did. So Valle retired on the spot and came home to Seattle to focus on helping the poor of the Dominican Republic. "Fame is fleeting, but the impact you make in the lives of others, to me, has eternal value," says Valle. "People don't forget those types of things."

Few can forget Dave Valle in the Dominican Republic, where the people know him as a man of true compassion. That compassion is demonstrated through Esperanza International, a nonprofit foundation Valle started in 1995, which has handed out more than two thousand loans to help poor Dominicans start small businesses. Unlike many athletes who pay lip service to charity and then disappear once the publicity dies, Valle is a hands-on participant in Esperanza, taking several trips a year to the Dominican Republic.

"When I tell you the setting most of these people survive in— dirt floors, cardboard and aluminum structures, no indoor plumbing—most people would not think they'd be a very good credit risk. But these women see these loans as an opportunity to make a better life for themselves and their kids."

Profile of Dave Valle

Esperanza means "hope" in Spanish, and that's just what the organization provides. Esperanza supplies loans, averaging $150, so Dominicans can begin to forge a way out of desperate poverty. The money goes almost exclusively to women, who are much more likely to use the money to help their families. According to Valle, the results have been spectacular. More than $300,000 has been lent, with a 96 percent on-time repayment rate, and most remarkable, no defaults. The women also receive training in accounting, business skills, and job training.

"When you give something to somebody and ask nothing in return, no responsibility, it actually robs them of their self-esteem," Valle said. "These women, they get their loan and repay it, and there's a sense of accomplishment they have. Their self-esteem rises, and then the possibilities for themselves are endless."

Valle talks of Ramona, "The Juice Woman," who used her loan to start a business providing juice drinks to her neighborhood. Other women prepare beans for restaurants or sell eggs at the market. "They say, 'Before, my children didn't eat every day. Now they eat every day. Now, they have shoes on their feet, where there were no shoes, and they have clothes on their back.'"

A number of major league players support Valle's vision, which was birthed when he was playing winter ball in 1985. "After games you would leave the park and literally see kids four and five years old begging for food," said Valle. "They were half-naked, most of them didn't have shoes. My wife and I said that if we were ever in a position to help people in that situation, we would."

"We've all made promises and forget about them in twenty-four hours," says foundation president Fred Gregory. "Dave and Vicky hung onto that dream and idea."

Valle is convinced that "if you really believe something, then it should cause you to live and act in a certain way."

Valle's example has rubbed off on his teenage son, Phillip. On one trip to Puerto Rico, at an orphanage, Valle saw his son trying to slip a dollar bill into a baby's diaper. "That's when I knew all of the lessons that I had been trying to teach him had sunk in," Valle said. "It's not your bank account or your job description, but what you do for other people that's important in life."

The Heart of a Champion looks for ways to help those in need:

Although he was a very solid catcher in his major league career, Dave Valle never gained a big name among the national baseball press. But among the people of the Dominican Republic, Valle is a champion. His work there has meant more than just throwing money at a glaring problem. Valle has committed not only his financial support but also his personal time to make a difference. Valle's understanding of personal value is based not on what he has but rather on what he gives.

What does it take for us to be moved to do something to help others? We are bombarded by emotional pitches on television and radio urging us to give money to help feed or clothe those in need. How often do we look away? "There is so much need," we say to ourselves, "what difference can I possibly make?" The answer, a lot. It all starts with one person, like Dave Valle, committed to making a difference.

We are not called to change the whole world. We're called to make a difference to one person. As Valle said, "It's not your bank account or your job description, but what you do for other people that's important in life." Do you have the same sense of value in your life? If not, then you need to find a place to contribute—with your money, or perhaps just your time. Give, and much more shall be given to you.

> *"Give, and it will be given to you. A good measure, pressed down, shaken together and running over, will be poured into your lap. For with the measure you use, it will be measured to you."*
>
> —Luke 6:38

Profile of JOHN WETTELAND

"He [John's neighbor] wanted me to help him with his pitching mechanics. I was sweating bullets, but I loved it. It was fun: pure, unadulterated baseball."

HUMILITY:

Champions know they are not above others.

One day during the 1997 season, then Texas Rangers star relief pitcher, John Wetteland, was about to leave for the ballpark when his doorbell rang. Wetteland found a young boy, maybe twelve years old, standing outside, nervously shifting from foot to foot.

"Is Mr. Wetteland here?" the boy asked.

"That's me," Wetteland replied.

Stammering, the boy asked if Wetteland could come outside and play catch.

Now, a lot of big leaguers would have brushed off the boy's request. But not Wetteland, who many teammates say is still a boy at heart himself.

There was, however, one problem: all his equipment was at The Ballpark at Arlington. "My wife and I searched the home for a glove and couldn't find one," Wetteland says. "I felt so bad. I told him, 'Look, I can't play now because I don't have a glove, but when I come back from the next road trip, I'll bring one home and we can play.'"

The boy wondered if Wetteland was just trying to get rid of him. A couple of weeks later the Rangers returned from a road trip, and the boy got his answer. As soon as he saw Wetteland at home, he once again asked the pitcher if he was up for a game of catch. Wetteland obliged. "We went out on the front lawn and played catch for about thirty minutes," Wetteland says. "He wanted me to help him with his pitching mechanics. I was sweating bullets, but I loved it. It was fun: pure unadulterated baseball."

The Heart of a Champion recognizes value in every person:

Think about John Wetteland's response to his neighbor. Every night for nine months, Wetteland was besieged by young fans seeking his autograph, a ball, a cap, a jersey—anything they could get their hands on. Some nights those same young fans catcalled and booed if he failed them. Yet a boy comes to the door wanting to play catch, and Wetteland jumps at the opportunity. In the era of the hedonistic athlete, John Wetteland played catch on the front lawn with a neighbor kid. It is a move to a different era; a scene right out of a Rockwell portrait, the way things ought to be. Wetteland understands that he is just an ordinary person with an extraordinary talent, no more important than the boy down the street. Because of that, this boy was worth an investment of his time.

Think about the eyes looking at you. What do they see in your responses? The so-called ordinary people in our lives—the woman in the checkout line, the man at the service station, the mail carrier, the newspaper deliverer. Too often we walk past people without giving them a thought. Are they worth your time and energy? If Jesus died for them, then they are worthy. The boy was affected by John Wetteland's compassion. What kind of effect are you having?

There is neither Jew nor Greek, slave nor free,
male nor female, for you are all one in Christ Jesus.

—Galatians 3:28

About the Author

Steve Riach is president and cofounder of VisionQuest Communications Group, Inc., a Dallas-based media company. Along with being a popular author and speaker, he is an award-winning producer, writer, and director of television and film projects, and is one of the nation's foremost creators of virtuous sports content. He is also cofounder of the Heart of a Champion Foundation, a nonprofit organization that has created an innovative program to teach character and virtue in schools. Steve and his family reside in Colleyville, Texas.

Heart of a Champion

The Heart of a Champion Foundation is an independent, national nonprofit organization utilizing the platform of sports to build and reinforce character and virtue in young people. Blending the message and the messenger, the Heart of a Champion Foundation's winning formula teaches and models character education at the grassroots level, to mold better citizens and develop the heart of a champion in youth.

The Heart of a Champion school program is a unique, in-class character education program that teaches positive character values and traits through video, audio, and written vignettes featuring popular and respected athletes and other individuals. Teaching virtues through "sight and sound" stories of positive role models attracts the attention of learners and arouses their interest, raising questions that lead to discussions and reflection about the implementation of those virtues into the daily life process. Stories that demonstrate values such as honesty, perseverance, courage, commitment, discipline, integrity, and fairness encourage students to recognize and follow their examples. The Heart of a Champion program also includes student, teacher, and parent enrichment materials to reinforce the positive character traits that are taught and discussed. The Heart of a Champion Foundation believes that teaching kids character and virtue can help build the champions of tomorrow through stories of the heroes of today. For more information, visit the Web site at www.heartofachampion.org, or call (972) 690-4588.

Heart of a Champion is a registered trademark under which virtuous sports products and programs are created and distributed. Materials include award-winning videos, television and radio programs, films, books, and Internet activities. To learn more about Heart of a Champion resources, products, or programming, call 972-690-4588, or visit the Web site at www.heartofachampion.org.

Additional copies of this and other
titles from Honor Books are available
wherever good books are sold.

Other devotional and gift book titles:

Passion for the Game
Above the Rim
The Drive to Win
Inspire a Dream
It's How You Play the Game
Life Lessons from Auto Racing
Life Lessons from Golf

If you have enjoyed this book,
or if it has had an impact on your life,
we would like to hear from you.

Please contact us at:

HONOR BOOKS
Cook Communications Ministries, Dept. 201
4050 Lee Vance View
Colorado Springs, CO 80918

Or visit our Web site:
www.cookministries.com

HONOR **HB** BOOKS

Inspiration and Motivation for the Seasons of Life